Introduction to

Prisons
and
Imprisonment

Nick Flynn has been deputy director of the Prison Reform Trust since 1994. As well as prisons—he has written widely on prison education and American sentencing policy—he has a background in training, employment and urban regeneration issues.

Introduction to
Prisons and Imprisonment

Published 1998 by
WATERSIDE PRESS
Domum Road
Winchester SO23 9NN
Telephone or Fax 01962 855567
INTERNET:106025.1020@compuserve.com

ISBN Paperback 1 872 870 37 6

Cataloguing-in-Publication Data A catalogue record for this book can be obtained from the British Library.

Printing and binding Antony Rowe Ltd, Chippenham

Cover design John Good Holbrook Ltd, Coventry. From original paintings by Peter Cameron: see below.

Peter Cameron started painting whilst serving a ten and a half year prison sentence and came to terms with his imprisonment by making it the subject of his art. He is now a freelance artist. For him, ironically, prison was a career move. He can be contacted at The Hub, 9-13 Berry Street, Liverpool. Telephone 0151 709 0889.

Introduction to

Prisons
and
Imprisonment

Nick Flynn

With a Foreword by

The Rt. Hon Lord Hurd of Westwell CH CBE PC

Under the auspices of the Prison Reform Trust

WATERSIDE PRESS
WINCHESTER

Introduction to
Prisons and Imprisonment

CONTENTS

Acknowledgements

I would like to thank the staff at the Prison Reform Trust. In particular Clare Sparks, Liz Seward, Diana Ruthven, Fiona Banatvala and Stephen Nathan, who all played their part in bringing this book to fruition. I would especially like to thank Stephen Shaw, director of the Prison Reform Trust, for spotting the howlers and improving my grammar and Julia Jackson, who, before leaving PRT, carried out much of the initial research.

This book is dedicated to my partner Jo and our son Jack. It is also dedicated to an old friend John. In a roundabout way, by serving four and a half years in Winson Green in the early 1980s, he got me involved in prison reform and made me realise that literally anyone can end up in prison, no matter how good natured or harmless.

Nick Flynn
September 1998

About the Prison Reform Trust

The Prison Reform Trust (PRT)
15 Northburgh Street, London EC1V 0JR. Tel. 0171 251 5070.
Fax. 0171 251 5076

The work of the Prison Reform Trust is aimed at creating a just, humane and effective penal system. It does this by: inquiring into the workings of the system; informing prisoners, staff, and the wider public; and by influencing Parliament, government and officials towards reform.

As well as publishing briefing papers, pamphlets and books on prisons PRT publishes a quarterly magazine, *Prison Report* and, with the Prison Service, the *Prisoners' Information Book*, a copy of which goes to every prisoner. In addition, *Prison Privatisation Report International* is published ten times a year.

Foreword

The debate about the prisons in this country becomes steadily more strenuous as the figures build up and overcrowding begins to undo much of the progress of recent years. Coming back to this scene after ten years doing other things, I am struck again by the large number of intelligent and committed people who are involved in and around prisons: magistrates, probation officers, Boards of Visitors, charities like the Prison Reform Trust, and of course the Prison Service itself. In all these organizations there is a wealth of experience and good sense, far removed from the caricature sometimes drawn of prison reformers as cloudy idealists.

Nevertheless the discussion within and between these groups is still limited. It does not usually spill out into the world inhabited by the media and by politicians. The press tend to pay attention to prisons only when there is a disaster such as a riot or a mass escape, or when some incident helps to recreate the myth that our prisons are palaces of leisure and comfort. A small handful of politicians take an interest, but such interest is regarded as eccentric, and I do not believe that a serving prime minister has ever visited a prison. Yet the purpose of prison, and what happens in prison, are themes of huge importance to our society. One of the aims of the Prison Reform Trust is to make the debate overflow into the minds of those who do not yet grasp the close connection between the state of our prisons and the state of society as a whole.

Nick Flynn is PRT's deputy director and this *Introduction to Prisons and Imprisonment* is typical of the approach which he has brought to the Trust and of the tone which he has helped us maintain. All of us involved in PRT have strong feelings about prisons. This is certainly true of Nick Flynn. But we do not feel that we can make progress by waving our arms and shouting out those opinions. Progress has to be based on a sober understanding of the facts of today, and the historical background to those facts. That is why the Prison Reform Trust devotes much of its energies to research, particularly in the United States and in Britain. Yes, we are a pressure group—pressing for the criminal justice system to pay more attention to valid alternatives to prison, pressing for decent regimes inside prisons with a stronger and clearer emphasis on education. But we want our arguments to be based on information soberly collected and dispassionately presented. That is why in this book Nick Flynn is not arguing a case for this or that reform. Instead he sets out the history, structure and characteristics of our prison system in a way which will be valuable not just to those who help to run that system but to everyone who understands its wider importance.

Too often imprisonment is thought of as the process by which magistrates and judges pluck out alien characters from our society and segregate them for the benefit of the rest of us. In reality prisoners are part of our society. They come from it and they will return to it. Their crimes and their case histories tell us something about that society. Seventy per cent of those held in the young offender institution at Feltham have fallen through our education system; they cannot effectively read, write or count. That failure of our education system does not excuse their criminality, but it certainly helps to explain it. So does the fact that half the women held in Holloway have serious drug problems.

When prison reformers cite such examples we are often accused of caring more for the offender than for the victim. But the fate of the offender and the victim are in practice closely linked. People are sent to prison because they are convicted or accused of a serious crime. If they are convicted, imprisonment is a punishment; if they are accused and awaiting trial then imprisonment is a precaution for the safety of the public. But in either case it is also something else. It is a period during which they have left behind their chaotic, undisciplined lives. They are told what to do and when to do it. They are given a glimpse, often inadequate, of the possibilities which work and education could offer them in the future. Then they are pushed back into the chaotic society from which they came. Will they create new victims? Will they be back in prison within weeks or months? The answer to those questions depends in part on the impact which prison made on their view of themselves.

That is why we do no service to the victim of crime by making a hash of our treatment of the offender; we simply prepare the fate of further victims. That is why, with the help of books like this one, the discussion of prisons and imprisonment needs to broaden out until it includes all those who are seriously interested in the punishment and prevention of crime.

Douglas Hurd
July 1998

CHAPTER 1

Introduction and Overview

There are currently 139 prisons in England and Wales. In mid-1998, the prison population was 65,652—the size of a small town, or a large football crowd. Prisoners are held in prison for two main reasons. Either because:

- they have been remanded to custody pending trial or sentence; or
- they have been convicted and sentenced by the courts to serve time in prison as a punishment.

This handbook describes the way the Prison Service operates in England and Wales, the staff who work for it, the prisoners who are held by it and the conditions and regimes to which they are subject. Although there are some basic similarities between prison systems throughout the world, there are also important differences in the way they are run and the functions they perform.

Even in countries as similar as Scotland, Northern Ireland and England and Wales, there are differences in the way that prison systems operate. The reasons for the differences are cultural, social and administrative. *Chapter 2* of this book describes the history of the prison system in England and Wales and the various events which have influenced its development. The hotch potch of prison buildings described in *Chapter 3*—some dating from medieval times, some positively futuristic in design—which comprise the prison estate today, is the legacy of this unique and varied history.

Prison conditions (*Chapter 5)* and prison regimes (*Chapter 6)* have been influenced by the attempts of many individuals to reform the prison system and by political and social pressures. Also the attitudes and characteristics of the prisoners themselves (*Chapter 4*) and the way that the Prison Service is organized and staffed (*Chapter 7*) play an important part in our understanding of how prisons function and have developed.

THE PURPOSE OF IMPRISONMENT

The maxim that history repeats itself can be most aptly applied to prisons. The fundamental questions asked about prisons today—what are they for and what should be done in them to reform offenders and deter potential offenders?—are the same questions that have been asked ever since imprisonment became the cornerstone of the penal system some two centuries ago. Yet, after more than 200 years of imprisoning offenders, we are no nearer to understanding why we do it.

It is possible to identify three different purposes of imprisonment:

- first, people who are awaiting trial and have been refused bail are imprisoned in order to prevent them from running away, committing further offences, or interfering with the due process of law. Prisons are also used to detain some asylum seekers and others believed to have breached immigration rules.

- second, imprisonment is used to enforce court orders such as fines, or community punishments like probation and community service. If offenders fail to comply with the conditions of such orders—for example, if they do not pay the fine or turn up for appointments with probation officers—they may be imprisoned as a punishment or as an alternative to the sanction originally imposed.

- third, imprisonment is used as a punishment in its own right. Prison as a punishment provides all societies with a response to crime and to the offenders who commit crime. There are other responses of course—cautions and warnings, fines and other financial penalties, punishments in the community, including the requirement to carry out voluntary work, or—in some countries— various forms of corporal and capital punishment. Most crime, insofar as it comes to the attention of the police and the offender is caught, is in fact punished in these other ways. Nevertheless, prison is always there as a back-up to these other penalties. In those countries which have abolished the death penalty, it is the maximum coercive sanction available to the state and it is the principal punishment for such serious crimes as drug-smuggling, robbery and sexual assaults.

In most countries, the various functions of imprisonment are usually divided between those which are symbolic in purpose and those which have a utilitarian value.

The symbolic purposes of imprisonment
By removing offenders from society and by imposing strict limitations on their freedom, imprisonment is intended to send a powerful symbolic message to offenders and potential offenders that criminal behaviour will not be tolerated. In this respect, imprisonment provides

a means for the state and the public to express its collective disapproval of criminal behaviour.

It is also frequently claimed, especially by those who support an increased use of imprisonment, that many people demand that offenders are sent to prison in the interests of retribution and revenge. Whatever the rights or wrongs of imposing punishments for such reasons, it is certainly the case that the criminal justice system exists in part to prevent vigilantism and people taking the law into their own hands.

The utilitarian purposes of imprisonment

The other set of arguments about the purpose of imprisonment concerns its role in reducing the incidence of crime. These utilitarian functions of imprisonment are usually divided into three: incapacitation, deterrence and rehabilitation.

Incapacitation: This is the common sense notion that offenders who are confined in prisons are rendered physically incapable of committing further crimes against the public for the length of their incarceration.

Deterrence: This is the idea that the threat of imprisonment discourages criminal behaviour and encourages people to abide by the rules of society. For those individuals who are not so influenced, longer, more frequent and harsher prison sentences must be imposed until they decide to give up their life of crime.

Rehabilitation: The third utilitarian function of prison is that it is intended to reform and rehabilitate offenders, whether by personal example, access to work, training and education, or through exposure to various types of treatment programme. By addressing the factors which are related to offending (lack of job, drug addiction, a hot temper, etc.) a positive prison regime can influence offenders to lead crime-free lives in the future.

It is through the repeated emphasising of these symbolic and utilitarian purposes of imprisonment that prison systems are maintained throughout the world. However, the symbolic power of imprisonment and the capacity of prison to reduce the incidence of crime are highly problematic concepts. Indeed, there are powerful counter arguments which suggest that, instead of reducing the incidence of crime, imprisonment can actually contribute to it.

13

'Universities of crime'

First, there is the universities of crime idea. This suggests that a consequence of confining offenders together is that they can all too easily influence each other to commit further crimes. Criminals make new contacts and learn new tricks. There is also some evidence that going to prison is seen as a rite of passage for some young criminals, a pre-condition to achieving status in street gangs and within the criminal fraternity.

On the other hand prison can also exert a powerful stigma on prisoners such that when they are released back into society they find it extremely difficult to adjust to a crime-free life-style. They may be spurned by their families and friends, and employers may be reluctant to offer them jobs. As a consequence, even those offenders who want to change their ways may drift back into a life of crime because they feel they have no other option.

The high cost of imprisonment

The function of imprisonment to incapacitate, deter, and rehabilitate offenders has also been questioned.

So far as incapacitation is concerned, most offenders are not in prison for very long and are free after a short while to resume their lives of crime. This is because the majority of offenders are imprisoned not for violent or sexual crimes, which attract long sentences, but for property offences, which normally attract much lower sentences; and because such crimes are usually the ones where the chances of arrest are lowest, imprisonment prevents very few extra offences from occurring.

Even if it were possible to prosecute more offenders and to imprison them for longer, the cost of building the extra prisons required to make a significant impact on the crime rate would be prohibitive. In this country, Home Office research has estimated that in order to reduce crime by one per cent, a 22 per cent increase in the use of custody would be required. The costs of building the new prisons to hold the extra numbers would run into billions of pounds.

Many crimes are unplanned

The theory of deterrence assumes that potential criminals carefully weigh up the risks, the costs and the benefits. But even if this were true, many potential offenders would not be deterred by the threat of imprisonment because they would know that only a small minority of offenders are successfully prosecuted and punished for their crimes. Their thinking would be 'If my friends can get away with it, why can't I?' Evidence from the *British Crime Survey* indicates that only two out of every 100 criminal offences result in an offender being sentenced by a

14

court and imprisoned. Therefore, the likelihood of conviction for committing an offence is so small that experienced offenders are unlikely to be deterred by the threat of imprisonment.

In any case, most crimes are not committed by people when they are at their most rational. Frequently, they are unplanned acts, spur of the moment offences, caused by anger or loss of temper. Many offences are also committed by people under the influence of drink or drugs, or by those suffering from mental health problems. It is difficult, therefore, to believe that they are thinking about the potential penalty when committing the crime. If they are not, then deterrence theory largely falls by the wayside.

'Nothing Works'

In terms of rehabilitation, there is little doubt that programmes and activities can help prisoners reform. But there is little evidence that such programmes work better in prisons than in the community. On the contrary, prison is a damaging experience. The rejection of rehabilitation as a justification for prison is grounded in the high reconviction rates for discharged prisoners. In this country, research has shown that 47 per cent of adult males and 40 per cent of females discharged from prison are convicted of further offences within two years. Reconviction rates for those under the age of 21 are higher still at 75 per cent for males and 51 per cent for females.

Although a considerable amount of research into the effectiveness of prison-based programmes and activities has been completed, much more needs to be done to demonstrate comprehensively how they work in practice. Indeed, until a few years ago, the consensus was that it did not matter what kind of programmes and activities were provided in prisons, since they all had only a limited effect. No treatment was better than any other, or than none at all. This became known as the 'Nothing Works' theory (see *Chapter 6*). Today, the consensus has shifted slightly and programmes which seek to address the offending behaviour of specific groups of prisoners are once again being developed in prisons. However, there remains a lack of good quality evidence to show how activities such as work, education and various offence-related treatment programmes may influence offenders to lead crime free lives in future.

RELATIONSHIP BETWEEN IMPRISONMENT AND CRIME RATES

As we have seen, supporters of an increased use of custody assert the incapacitative and deterrent effects of imprisonment. They argue that longer and more frequent prison sentences protect the public by taking offenders out of circulation and by deterring criminals and potential criminals from offending. To support their arguments they say there is a direct relationship between an increase in the prison population and a reduction in crime.

For example, in the United States of America, according to the FBI crime index, there was a 13 per cent decline in the overall crime rate between 1991 and 1995, which included a 22 per cent decline in the violent crime rate and an 11 per cent decline in the property crime rate. In this country, between 1992 and 1996 total recorded crime fell by ten per cent, although total recorded violent crime during the same period rose by 21 per cent. In both countries these falls have coincided with an increase in the prison population.

Opponents of the view that imprisonment has a significant effect on crime argue, however, that there is no evidence of a direct link between falling crime rates and an increased use of custody. They point to the importance of other factors such as changes in demography, especially the numbers of young people in the population, the introduction of new policing methods and increasing prosperity. They argue that crime figures are unreliable, they fluctuate over time and that it is simplistic to assume that a dip in crime over a short period of time is a direct consequence of harsher sentencing practice.

They argue that, although there has been a recent reduction in recorded crime in England and Wales, total recorded crime today is 31 per cent higher than it was ten years ago and since 1979 the number of crimes recorded by the police has risen by 121 per cent. Finally, they point to the high cost of imprisonment and the effect of holding increasing number of prisoners on the quality of prison regimes.

DIFFERENCES IN CULTURAL AND SOCIAL ATTITUDES TOWARDS IMPRISONMENT

The use of imprisonment differs from country to country and is prone to change over time. To some extent, such differences are related to the varying levels of crime experienced in different countries. However, differing attitudes towards imprisonment are not necessarily related to fluctuations in crime rates, or to the number of offenders coming before the courts. The use of imprisonment appears to be dependent as much on cultural and social factors. Moreover, politicians and the media can both strongly influence the public mood.

International comparisons

The differences in cultural and social attitudes towards imprisonment throughout the world were revealed as recently as 1996. An International Crime Victimisation Survey reported that, in many western European countries, it was punishments delivered in the community, rather than imprisonment, that were most favoured by the public for repeat burglars. On the other hand, public support for imprisonment was greatest in the United Kingdom and in the United States of America.

Comparing countries' use of imprisonment is not easy. Definitions of 'prison' are not standard; and in some countries—China, for example—the official statistics cannot be trusted.

The available figures indicate that Russia, which has an imprisonment rate of around 690 per 100,000 of the population, is the country which relies most heavily on imprisonment. This is in keeping with high rates recorded in other Eastern European countries, especially those which were formerly part of the Soviet Union. Next comes the United States of America which imprisons around 615 per 100,000 of its population. Throughout Europe, only Portugal currently gaols more offenders than the United Kingdom. England and Wales currently imprisons offenders at a rate of over 120 per 100,000 of the population, compared to 89 in France, 84 in Germany, 67 in Holland, 65 in Sweden, 60 in the Republic of Ireland, Norway, Finland, Greece and 58 in Switzerland.

Changes in attitudes over time

Political support for harsher sentencing practices and, consequently, an increased use of imprisonment, can influence both the courts and public opinion. For example, in America during the 1980s, President Reagan introduced legislation which had the effect of increasing the frequency and length of prison sentences imposed by the courts. And because similar policies have been pursued by both President Bush and President Clinton, the prison population in state and federal prisons throughout America increased from 329,821 at the beginning of the 1980s to over 1.6 million by 1996—a rise of 385 per cent.

In the United Kingdom, between 1993 and 1997 the then home secretary, Michael Howard, pursued a policy of increasing the prison population in the belief that 'prison works'. In other words, that the most effective way of dealing with criminals was to lock them up. This represented a reversal of previous policy which had sought to reduce the prison population by systems of early release (see *Chapter 2*) and by increasing the range of community penalties available to the courts. As a consequence, after falling by 3,327 between 1987 and 1990, the prison

17

population increased in England and Wales from 40,606 at the end of 1992 to 62,481 by September 1996—an increase of 54 per cent.

Michael Howard's ability to 'talk up' the prison population by influencing sentencers to impose prison sentences more frequently is revealed by the fact that between 1992 and 1996, at all courts, the proportion of those sentenced to custody for indictable offences rose from 16 per cent to 23 per cent. At Crown Courts, the proportion rose from 46 per cent to 63 per cent; and at magistrates' courts, it doubled from five to ten per cent. During the same period, the average length of sentences also increased for virtually all categories of offence. (Normally, you would expect the average length of sentence to fall if the use of imprisonment rose.)

The shift in policy which took place under Michael Howard was only the latest of many changes in the way that crime has been tackled over the years. Throughout the century, claims and counter claims concerning the overall purpose of imprisonment have resulted in major disagreements about how prisons should be run and what they are for. The consequence is that consensus on the purpose of imprisonment has never been reached in England and Wales. Indeed, *Chapter 7*, which describes the current management structure of the Prison Service, shows that disagreement over such a fundamental item as the wording of the Prison Service statement of purpose remains an active issue.

The most recent *British Crime Survey* in 1996 found that, rather than support an increased use of imprisonment, the majority of people tended to be sceptical about its overall effectiveness to reduce crime. When asked to identify the best ways of tackling crime, 36 per cent of respondents cited an increase in family discipline and 25 per cent selected a reduction in unemployment. Only one fifth opted for harsher sentencing. This survey found that attitudes towards a greater use of imprisonment were mixed, with a widespread belief that imprisonment can stimulate as well as prevent further crime. Far more people expressed a preference for tougher community penalties than for building new prisons as a means of tackling prison overcrowding. In conclusion, the authors of the survey accused politicians of 'playing to the gallery' by supporting criminal justice policies which pander to the public's mistaken appetite for tougher punishments. They also blamed the media for spreading misleading stories about levels of crime and the conduct of the courts.

THE CURRENT CRISIS

Under such circumstances, it is perhaps unsurprising that the problems facing the Prison Service in England and Wales today—overcrowding, poor staff morale, enforced idleness amongst prisoners, high rates of re-offending—are the same problems that were wrestled over by prison administrators during the Victorian age. That is not to deny there have been some important improvements. Prisoners are no longer kept for long periods in solitary confinement and made to 'purge their souls' by performing meaningless and degrading tasks. Bribery and corruption has been removed from the system; bread-and-water diets and flogging have been abolished; sanitation in prisons has been upgraded; security has been tightened; prisons built during the past 15 years offer facilities of a much higher standard than those available in those built in Victorian times; and prisoners now have greater access to activities in prison, such as work and education.

However, despite over a century of concern about prison conditions and of devising various means to improve practice, the prison system remains beset by a number of intractable problems.

Prison overcrowding

Perhaps the biggest problem facing the Prison Service today is prison overcrowding. The causes of prison overcrowding are obvious. As it is the duty of the Prison Service to keep in custody all those offenders committed by the courts, that service must try to balance the supply of prison accommodation with the demand for places. When resources do not keep pace with a rise in numbers, prisons become overcrowded.

The table opposite shows that since the Second World War the relationship between prison numbers has been out of kilter with prison capacity on an almost constant basis. Between 1945 and the mid-1960s, the prison population increased from around 15,000 to over 30,000. Prisons became increasingly overcrowded, such that by the end of 1968, over 5,000 prisoners were 'trebled up'—three men living in cells designed for one.

At the beginning of 1998, the prison population was 62,115, having increased by over ten per cent during the previous year. The rise in numbers has affected some groups of prisoners more than others. Since 1992, the rise in the number of women prisoners has been twice as rapid as that for males. In February 1998, the women's prison population exceeded 3,000 for the first time since 1905, having increased by 30 per cent since mid-September 1996 when it was 2,339 and by 124 per cent since the end of 1992 when it was 1,353.

Of no less consequence, the effects of overcrowding have not been spread evenly across the country. Because overcrowding tends to be concentrated in the local and remand prisons, many of which date from the nineteenth century, it is unconvicted and unsentenced prisoners who are made to suffer the worst conditions. During 1997, local prisons

19

were 25 per cent over capacity on average. And some were much more overcrowded than this. At the end of July 1997, ten local prisons were over 40 per cent overcrowded. Birmingham was 46 per cent over capacity; Dorchester 56 per cent; Leicester 64 per cent; Canterbury 69 per cent; Northallerton 74 per cent; and Shrewsbury 83 per cent overcrowded.

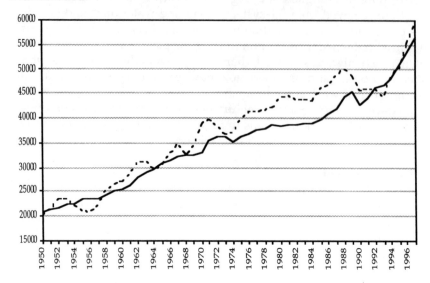

———— Certified Normal Accommodation   ⋯⋯ Average Prison Population

Prison Overcrowding 1950 to 1997

Source: Home Office

An *Audit of Prison Service Resources*, carried out by the incoming Labour government and published on 25 July 1997, revealed that the prison population is expected to rise to at least 68,900 by March 2000. The audit showed that by the financial year 2001-02, the shortfall between the number of prisoners and the capacity of the Prison Service to accommodate prisoners in uncrowded conditions (the 'certified normal accommodation') is forecast to be 11,600. The shortfall between the number of prisoners and the maximum useable capacity with overcrowding (the 'operational capacity') is forecast to be 3,300.

On the date of its publication, the new home secretary, Jack Straw, spelled out the consequences of the findings in the audit for the immediate future of the Prison Service:

In the three months since the election, [the prison population] has risen by 2,440, far exceeding any projection published before May 1. This three-month rise is equivalent to the total capacity of four average-sized prisons . . . The building programme approved by the previous government is already being outstripped by the rise in population, which on latest assumptions will exceed maximum capacity later this year, and will do so again by a larger margin by early 1999. The number of prisoners 'doubled' — held two to a cell designed for one — has already increased from 7,251 in 1992 to 10,926 at the end of June and, on current plans, would have to increase to around 16,000 by early 1999; meanwhile, the level of purposeful activity for prisoners has dropped over the last two years, so limiting the scope for reducing the risk of prisoners re-offending on release.

He added that

. . . there is a growing risk of prisons having to close because heating, electrical and water systems, roofs and other infrastructure have not been adequately maintained.

The prison building programme

In 1991, the Woolf Inquiry, which was set up to establish the causes of the prison riots which swept through over 20 prisons the previous year (see *Chapter 2*) stressed that in order to avoid overcrowding, the best possible information should be used to plan the prison building programme. It reported that

It must be recognised that it is the duty of society and therefore of the government of the day to provide the resources necessary to accommodate all prisoners in humane and acceptable conditions. Since such conditions cannot be produced quickly, the fulfilment of this duty requires careful planning based on the best possible projections of the likely prison population.

The fact that the prison system continues to suffer so badly from overcrowding suggests that in recent years the best possible projections have not been used to plan for future accommodation needs, or that the best possible projections are inaccurate. Between 1979 and 1995, 28 new prisons were opened, compared to 13 which were taken out of use. However, the additional accommodation that has been created has not been sufficient to meet the demand for places from the courts and the Prison Service is now having to introduce emergency measures to cope.

These include erecting new quick assembly house blocks and what are known as 'Ready-to-Use' units, within the perimeter walls of existing prisons. In addition, a prison ship was purchased from the New York Department of Corrections and opened on 11 June 1997 as HMP The Weare, moored in Portland Harbour, near Weymouth. The government is also believed to be investigating plans to adapt various types of existing accommodation, such as former military bases and holiday camps, for prison use. In February 1998, Jack Straw announced that an extra £70 million, on top of £43 million pledged the previous July, would be made available to the Prison Service to create 4,820 new prison places, in addition to the existing prison building programme.

Cuts in prison expenditure

At the same time as the prison population has been rising, there has been a significant reduction in the Prison Service operating budget. Between 1995-96 and 1996-97 prisons reduced their unit costs by three per cent and further reductions were planned for 1997-98 and 1998-99. Although any public service which consumes over £1.8 billion of public money needs to carefully consider its spending decisions, a reduction in the prison budget has serious implications. Unless productivity improves, it causes prison conditions to deteriorate and it decreases the amount of work that can be done with prisoners to help them lead crime-free lives after release.

Industrial relations

Industrial relations in prisons have had a troubled history. Not only do prison staff determine the atmosphere in prisons, in many respects they also determine whether management is able to implement changes in prison policy. By removing their support and refusing to cooperate, prison staff can hamper the progress of new initiatives and obstruct reforms. The interests of prison staff are represented by a number of trades unions, the two most important of which are the Prison Officers Association (POA) and the Prison Governors Association (PGA).

In 1997, the POA represented approximately 28,500 members including some governors, most prison officers, auxiliaries and storemen. First established in the 1930s, the POA today is considered by many to be one of the last of the old style trade unions and, through its organization of branches in every prison, is able to command a powerful sense of loyalty from its members.

Technically, industrial action in prisons is unlawful. In practice, there are a variety of ways in which staff can 'work to rule', causing disruption as a result.

The Prison Governors Association was established in 1987 to represent the views of prison governors on professional issues as well as trade union negotiations. Over the years, the PGA has steadily increased its membership so that it now represents nearly 90 per cent of all possible members. It has spoken out on a number of professional

22

issues, such as the effects of overcrowding, and has developed policy positions on many developments in penal policy.

Most recently, the POA has opposed decisions of the Labour government to extend private contracts for the management of prisons and to award new ones. The union has also continued to press for restoration of full trade union rights, including the right to take lawful industrial action. Although the POA has lost some of its muscle, industrial relations in prisons continue to be marked by disagreements at local and national level.

Security

A primary goal of any prison system is to ensure prisoners do not escape and to maintain a safe environment for both prisoners and staff. However, in recent years a number of serious lapses in prison control and security have shaken the confidence of the public in the ability of the Prison Service in England and Wales to ensure the safe and secure custody of offenders. Following the riot at Strangeways prison in Manchester and at 20 other prisons throughout the country in 1990, the escape of eight high security prisoners from HMP Whitemoor and HMP Parkhurst in 1993 and 1994, along with the subsequent discovery of semtex explosive at HMP Whitemoor (see *Chapter 2*), the work of the Prison Service has come under the most intense scrutiny. Such incidents have triggered almost continuous administrative restructuring and reform as one review of practice has succeeded another. Events reached a head in 1995 when the then director general of the Prison Service, Derek Lewis, was sacked by Michael Howard.

Quite apart from causing great confusion within the Prison Service, the two main inquiries into prison security have resulted in recommendations that have been implemented at great public expense. The Woodcock and Learmont inquiries into the escapes from Whitemoor and Parkhurst have been criticised for being applied too broadly and for severely distorting the pattern of Prison Service spending. Outrage followed revelations that pregnant women prisoners had been shackled to hospital beds up to the point of giving birth at the beginning of 1996, an indication of how far the policy of greater security had been taken.

Speaking in 1996, Derek Lewis, said:

> I believe . . . the public has a right to know whether the top management of the Prison Service believes that all the security recommendations in the Woodcock and Learmont reports make operational sense and whether the huge expenditures really offer the taxpayer good value for money. Prison escapes have already been reduced by 83 per cent in the last three decades and are still falling. The number of escapes by Category A prisoners is tiny

23

and they are generally caused by a failure to follow procedures, not a lack of resources.

As far as possible, the cost savings that have been made recently have been shared across the Prison Service as a whole. Compulsory redundancies have been avoided in favour of an early retirement package and over 1,000 members of staff accepted offers of early retirement or severance. However, as cost savings are made with the retirement of older staff, this has resulted in the loss of more experienced officers, and in some cases the replacement of full-time officers by auxiliaries and part-time staff. In 1996, a quarter of all prison governors applied for voluntary redundancy.

Overall, between 1993 and 1997, the number of new staff recruited to the Prison Service did not keep pace with the rise in the number of prisoners. The number of prison officers in post decreased from 23,994 to 23,058 and the ratio of all prison staff to prisoners rose from 1:1.17 to 1:1.50.

Prison conditions
Overcrowding is a major cause of deterioration in prison conditions. It also means that many prisoners have to be held in prisons situated long distances from their home areas, making it extremely difficult for family and friends to visit. It decreases the amount of time prisoners are able to spend out of their cells; and it causes relationships between prisoners and staff to deteriorate.

In 1990, the then director general of the Prison Service, Christopher Train, described to the Woolf Inquiry the damaging effect overcrowding has on prison conditions:

> The life and work of the Prison Service have, for the last 20 years, been distorted by the problem of overcrowding. That single factor has dominated pressure on staff, and as a consequence has soured industrial relations . . . The removal of overcrowding is . . . an indispensable pre-condition of sustained and universal improvement in prison conditions . . . the canker of overcrowding must be rooted out.

The Woolf Report was so concerned about the damaging effects of overcrowding on prison life that it recommended that no prison should hold more prisoners than was allowed by its certified normal accommodation, unless it had the express permission of Parliament to do so. However, the idea of a 'cap' on prison overcrowding was rejected by the government as unworkable. Prison conditions today are markedly better than at the time of the Strangeways riot and the Woolf Inquiry. They are lighter, airier, cleaner. However, recent reports of HM

24

Chief Inspector of Prisons show how poor conditions still obtain in many gaols:

HMP Northallerton in Yorkshire

Overcrowding drafts are having to be received from as far away as Wales, with all the implications this has for families. The end result of this is that the bulk of the population is locked up and idle.

HMP Highpoint in Suffolk

I have to ask how Highpoint has been allowed to deteriorate in the way that it has . . . a working week of 14.5 hours, more than 150 prisoners without meaningful occupation, the slashing of the education budget . . . the absence of any PE at weekends . . . the absence of any sort of anti-bullying policy . . . There is only one way to describe each of these — unacceptable.

HMP Littlehey in Cambridgeshire

Littlehey encapsulates the problems facing the Prison Service today, and the contents of this report will make a depressingly familiar read . . . Increasing numbers meaning that too many prisoners in training prisons are short of work . . . Offending behaviour programmes showing signs of having lost their way. Low staff morale . . . and so on, and so on.

Feltham YOI in London

Feltham is bursting at the seams. It is not an institution able to tackle re-offending . . . but a gigantic transit camp, in which day-to-day activities are dominated by the process of finding beds for ever increasing numbers, particularly of young remand prisoners, and ensuring they get to court on time.

HMP Wormwood Scrubs in London

Quite frankly, I was both surprised and horrified to find conditions at HMP Wormwood Scrubs to be as bad as they were . . . Much of the accommodation was dirty, for which there is no excuse. The regime for all but a small proportion of prisoners was impoverished. Some of the worst conditions, and the poorest regime, were endured by prisoners on remand, many of whom will be found not guilty of the offences for which they are charged.

HMP Lincoln

Anyone reading either paragraph 3.01, which describes A [the Remand] Wing, where prisoners inflict a high level of assaults on one another and bullying is endemic, and paragraph 3.03 which details that on the Wing around 200 prisoners were being unlocked every day, with little constructive activity to keep them occupied, must be alarmed. When you go on to read paragraph 3.35 which describes conditions in the first night centre—no natural light on the ground floor; cells in a dreadful state; mattresses ripped and stained; toilet seats broken; graffiti on cell walls dating back over two years; remains of encrusted and old food stuck to the walls of a cell—you begin to wonder in which country, and in what century, what is described is being allowed to take place. When you then realise that it is England in 1997 you feel angry that this is being tolerated . . .

Prison suicides

Perhaps the starkest evidence that prison life is far from being the holiday camp it is sometimes portrayed as is the fact that the number of prisoners taking their own lives has increased steadily for the past seven years. In spite of the introduction of new procedures by the Prison Service which seek to meet the needs of prisoners who may be vulnerable to suicide, the number of prison suicides increased from 50 in 1990 to 70 in 1997. It is difficult to attribute a single cause to the increase and the fact that there has been a steady rise in the number of suicides amongst young men within the general population is undoubtedly a factor. However, it is also true that overcrowding, and the various operational pressures that stem from it, means that the Prison Service is less equipped to deal with the day-to-day needs of vulnerable prisoners.

Prison regimes

Since the Prison Service became a Next Steps agency of government (see *Chapter 7*), prison governors have enjoyed more devolved responsibility for managing their budgets and customising regimes to local needs and requirements. As a consequence, decisions on how to achieve the cuts in prison expenditure at a local level have been left to individual governors. Many governors have been left with little choice but to cut prisoner programmes and activities in order to make the required savings.

Overall, prisoners now spend more time locked in their cells and less time engaged in constructive activity than they did in the mid-1990s. As highlighted by the *Audit of Prison Service Resources*, 1997, 'the level of purposeful activity for prisoners has dropped over the last two years, so limiting the risk of prisoners re-offending on release'. Between 1994-95 and 1996-97, the percentage of prisoners allowed out of their cells for an average of more than ten hours per day fell from 70 per cent to 60 per cent; and the average number of weekly hours spent by prisoners in constructive activity fell from 26.2 to 23.8.

Education

Between 1995-96 and 1996-97, 71 per cent of prisons reduced the level of education provided to prisoners. Nationally, the average number of hours per week prisoners spent in education fell from 1.8 hours in June 1995 to 1.5 hours in the second quarter of 1997. In some prisons the cuts have been more drastic. In HMP Wandsworth, for example, the number of education hours was cut by more than half between 1995-96 and 1996-97. In addition, the core curriculum of courses provided has been reduced to the teaching of a small number of core skills including basic literacy, numeracy, life and social skills, and information technology.

Writing in 1996, two teachers employed at HMP Pentonville warned of the consequences of cutting education for the Prison Service:

> This is a crisis situation. We are about to lose 40 per cent of our education classes within a few weeks. The education budget at Pentonville has been cut from £300,000 to £180,000, which means a reduction in annual teaching hours from 10,884 to 5,806. The second part of the Prison Service mission statement is to 'help prisoners lead law abiding lives in custody and after release'. This is being ignored. The knock-on effects will not only increase the already worsening tension at Pentonville, but will ultimately lead to angrier, and possibly more dangerous, prisoners being set free.

Offence related programmes

Budget cuts have also resulted in a slowing of the development of offence-related programmes. While the Prison Service has protected courses which have been accredited as demonstrating that they have a positive effect on prisoners' offending behaviour, these remain extremely few in number. In 1996-97, a total of 1,373 prisoners completed offence-related programmes, of whom 663 completed the Sex Offender Treatment Programme. This figure represents about two per cent of the average prison population and far less than two per cent of the annual throughput of prisoners.

PROBATION IN PRISON

Like education, probation services in prison have suffered as a result of the cuts. During 1996-97, 38 per cent of prisons reduced the numbers of probation officers who are seconded to prisons to help prisoners prepare for their release. Between June 1995 and December 1996, the number of probation officers in prisons was reduced by 16 per cent from 645 to 543.

SO WHAT OF THE FUTURE?

In the run up to the last general election in May 1997, both the Labour and Conservative parties were keen to demonstrate their 'tough' law and order credentials to the electorate. In a 'war of soundbites', the Labour party slogan 'tough on crime and tough on the causes of crime' was pitted against the former prime minister, John Major's exhortation that where criminals are concerned 'we should understand a little less, and condemn a little more'.

In power, the new Labour government has implemented parts of the Crime (Sentences) Act 1997, introduced by the previous Conservative government, which provides mandatory minimum sentences for certain categories of offence (see *Chapter 2*). This has been interpreted as a sign that Labour is prepared to sanction an increasing prison population. However, the government has also had to come to terms with a prison system which is already bursting at the seams. A more pragmatic approach has therefore also been in evidence.

For example, given the pressures on prison capacity and resources, the government decided not to implement the provisions of the Crime (Sentences) Act which would have introduced three year mandatory prison sentences for offenders convicted of domestic burglary for a third time. This was because Home Office estimates had suggested that implementation would have increased the prison population by some 3,000 per year. The government has also announced new contracts for privately managed prisons, despite voicing vociferous opposition towards them while in opposition (see *Chapter 3*). Now they are in power, day-to-day operational problems of how to balance numbers and resources, how to improve prison conditions and regimes with a limited expenditure and how to ensure prisons remain safe and secure are the pressing ones for New Labour.

CHAPTER 2

History of Imprisonment in England and Wales

Imprisonment—the lawful denial of liberty—has existed since the Roman era and perhaps before. But it is only relatively recently that prisons have been thought of as places of punishment. Until the beginning of the eighteenth century, prisons were used primarily as places to hold suspects awaiting trial, exile or execution, or to enforce the payment of debts.

The first real prisons in the modern sense—local gaols, 'houses of correction', or 'bridewells' as they were variously known—were administered on a local basis usually by magistrates. They were used to confine prisoners awaiting trial or execution of a sentence, debtors, vagrants and other petty offenders who had committed various 'crimes against morality'.

EARLY PRISON CONDITIONS

In 1777, John Howard, a former Sheriff of Bedfordshire, described early prison conditions in his influential book, *The State of the Prisons in England and Wales.* He found them, 'filthy, corrupt-ridden and unhealthy'. During inspections of prisons, carried out in England and later throughout the rest of Europe, Howard found prisoners held together in appalling conditions, irrespective of their age, sex, or whether they were tried or untried. He discovered poor standards of sanitation which helped spread diseases, such as typhus. He also criticised corrupt gaolers who, because they received no payment, made their living by charging prisoners for board and lodging.

Despite the efforts of Howard and other early penal reformers, attempts to improve conditions for prisoners were piecemeal. However, the spread of 'gaol fever' (louse-borne typhus) to the outside world did encourage improvements in health and hygiene. At this time imprisonment existed alongside other punishments—notably floggings, executions and transportation.

Transportation
Transportation was widely used during the eighteenth and first half of the nineteenth century. Requiring considerable investment and central

29

planning, transportation was seen both as social cleansing and as a harsh, deterrent penalty.

Initially, convicts were transported to the Americas. Between 1718 and 1775 some 30,000 convicts were transported to the West Indies and North America for periods of between seven and 14 years. Transportation was interrupted after the end of the American War of Independence in 1776, but resumed when the colonisation of Australia began in 1787. Some 160,000 convicts were transported to Australia over a period of 80 years, the majority being sent there after the Napoleonic wars had ended in 1815.

Prison ships
Requiring an alternative to transportation after the American War of Independence, Parliament passed an Act in 1779 which introduced the new punishment of hard physical labour. An early form of hard labour, which had much practical appeal, required convicts to dredge navigation channels in the River Thames. As a means of confining convicts close to their places of work, old sailing ships, or 'hulks', as they came to be known, were brought back into service. The hulks were also used for those awaiting transportation to Australia. Because they eased the pressures of overcrowding in local gaols they became more widely used, such that by 1828 there were ten hulks anchored along the Thames and at Plymouth and Portsmouth, which held a total of 4,446 convicts. However, the slow realisation that conditions on the hulks were appalling—initially about one third of the convicts died on them—and that they were breeding grounds for crime and corruption, finally led Parliament to discontinue their use in 1857.

Penitentiaries
Gradually, as imprisonment became a more accepted part of penal practice—public floggings were abolished in 1862 and transportation was finally abandoned in 1868—conditions in local gaols and houses of correction became the subject of closer scrutiny.

The appalling state of prisons had received official recognition for the first time in 1810 when the Holford Committee was established by Parliament to provide a forum for debate on imprisonment. A practical outcome of the Committee was the decision to build a national penitentiary at Millbank in central London. Completed in 1816, the Millbank penitentiary became the first prison to attempt to reform prisoners through a system of solitary confinement and rigorous religious instruction. It held over 1,000 prisoners, employed about 80 staff, including a chaplain, a schoolteacher and a surgeon, and provoked much public discussion at the time.

During this time attempts were made to reduce the harm of imprisonment and to ensure greater uniformity of practice in prisons. In 1823, the home secretary, Sir Robert Peel, initiated the Gaol Act which sought to divide prisoners according to the crimes they had committed and whether they might respond to efforts to reform them. In practice, however, the means of containing each category of prisoner proved to be remarkably similar.

A little later, the Prisons Act 1835 provided for the appointment of five inspectors of prisons and an Act of 1844 authorised the appointment of a Surveyor General of Prisons and introduced guidelines for the building of new prisons. By 1850, influenced by the experiment at Millbank, 20 new prisons had been authorised, all of which functioned as penitentiaries. The most famous of these, Pentonville, contained 520 prisoners, all of whom were kept in solitary confinement for as long as 18 months. All communication between prisoners and staff was forbidden and prisoners attended chapel and exercised separately. This enforced isolation was supposed to ensure prisoners had ample time and opportunity to reflect on the error of their ways.

Establishment of the Prison Commission
The Prisons Act 1877 transferred responsibility for prisons from local justices of the peace to the home secretary. Administration of the new system was delegated to a Prison Commission, which was charged with instilling greater uniformity and efficiency into the running of all prisons.

Sir Edmund Du Cane
The first Head of the Prison Commission was Sir Edmund Du Cane, a former officer of the Royal Engineers. His first action was to close just under half of the 113 local prisons in order to cut costs. A firm believer in punishment over reformation, Du Cane ensured that prison life was characterised by what became known as 'hard labour, hard board and hard fare'. All prisoners were kept in solitary confinement, given closely cropped hair cuts and made to wear regulation clothing emblazoned with broad arrows.

Scientists were appointed to advise on the quantity of hard labour that could be extracted from prisoners and the amount of food they required in order to maintain basic standards of human existence. Much of the work was useless and monotonous and included turning treadwheels and cranks for no purpose other than to exact punishment. Slightly more practical activities, although no less monotonous, included sewing mailbags, stone breaking and 'picking oakum' (removing fibres from old ropes to caulk boats). Oscar Wilde refers to this painful process in *The Ballad of Reading Gaol:*

We tore the tarry rope to shreds
With blunt and bleeding nails;
We rubbed the doors, and scrubbed the floors,
And cleaned the shining rails:
And, rank by rank, we soaped the plank,
and clattered with the pails.

We sewed the sacks, we broke the stones,
We turned the dusty drill:
We banged the tins, and bawled the hymns,
And sweated on the mill:
But in the heart of every man
Terror was lying still.

The Gladstone Committee

Du Cane's emphasis on the deterrent value of imprisonment provoked considerable criticism from penal reformers who pointed to the high numbers of offenders who continued to offend after their release. Of more immediate concern to Parliament however, was the fact that solitary confinement was becoming more and more impractical because of the increasing numbers of prisoners coming into the system.

In 1895 the government responded by establishing a Parliamentary Committee on prisons. Chaired by Herbert Gladstone, the son of the prime minister William Gladstone, the Gladstone Committee challenged Du Cane's emphasis on punishment and advocated a more reformative approach to imprisonment.

Arguing that all prisoners are different and that hard labour on its own was ineffective in reforming criminal behaviour, the Committee proposed that

... the system should be made more elastic, more capable of being adopted to the special cases of individual prisoners . . . treatment should be more effectively designed to maintain, stimulate or awaken the higher susceptibilities of prisoners, to develop their moral instincts, to train them in orderly and industrial habits, and whenever possible to turn them out of prison better men and women, both physically and morally, than when they came in.

In more specific terms, the Committee recommended that visiting entitlements for prisoners should be extended, a reformatory for young offenders should be established and after-care services be made available to prisoners after release. The subsequent Prisons Act 1898 officially abolished hard labour and introduced a classification system

32

for prisoners according to age, sex and whether they were convicted or unconvicted.

Although many of the recommendations would not be realised until well into the next century, the Gladstone Committee would prove to be a landmark in the development of the prison system in England and Wales. In stressing the role of the prison system to 'turn [prisoners] out of prison better physically and morally than when they came in', the Gladstone Committee endorsed the twin priorities of deterrence and rehabilitation, which underpin the function of the Prison Service today.

THE TWENTIETH CENTURY

From 1900 onwards a more optimistic and progressive attitude towards imprisonment emerged. In 1910, the then home secretary, Winston Churchill, summed up the new mood in a speech to Parliament, which has been quoted widely ever since. He said

A calm, dispassionate recognition of the rights of the accused, and even of the convicted criminal against the state; a constant heart-searching by all charged with the duty of punishment; a desire and eagerness to rehabilitate in the world of industry those who have paid their due in the hard coinage of punishment; tireless efforts towards the discovery of curative and regenerative processes; unfailing faith that there is a treasure, if you can find it, in the heart of every man; these are the symbols which, in the treatment of crime and criminals, mark and measure the stored-up strength of a nation, and are sign and proof of the living virtue in it.

Sir Evelyn Ruggles-Brise
Between 1895 and 1921, the next Head of the Prison Commission, Sir Evelyn Ruggles-Brise, presided over a gradual improvement in the administrative efficiency of prisons. The English system, Ruggles-Brise observed, '. . . insists on order and obedience and cleanliness and industry, as a primary and essential condition of imprisonment'. During his term of office, separate confinement was phased out. Prisoners were no longer required to keep their hair cropped short. Prison industries were introduced. Prisoners were issued with notebooks and pencils. Medical facilities were improved and levels of hygiene raised.

Sir Alexander Paterson
After the First World War, a gathering consensus that the overriding purpose of imprisonment was reformation of the prisoner began to assert itself. Most significantly, the view that 'Men are sent to prison as a punishment, not for punishment'—expressed by Sir Alexander Paterson, who served as a prison commissioner between 1922 and

1945—influenced the development of a number of initiatives which were intended to reform criminal behaviour. Paterson, a deeply religious man, who had spent 20 years of his life working as a voluntary social worker, is chiefly remembered for his introduction of borstals, which he presented as a combination of prison and the public school, and promoted to the general public as a distinctly English invention.

Borstals

Named after a village in Kent where the first one was built, borstals attempted to instil trust and responsibility and a sense of patriotic duty towards king and country in young offenders. They consisted of house blocks, each of which had a housemaster who encouraged participation in sport and recreational activities. As Paterson himself explained, the borstal system was

> based on the double assumption that there is individual good in each, and among nearly all an innate corporate spirit which will respond to the appeal made to the British of every sort to play the game, follow the flag, and stand by the old ship.

Now regarded as a somewhat quaint and naive product of a bygone age—they were abandoned formally in 1982—the principles which underpinned borstals nevertheless carried over into adult prisons and, to some extent, have influenced the development of the prison system ever since.

Open prisons

Paterson's belief that 'you cannot train a man for freedom under conditions of captivity', led to the opening of three borstals, at Lowdham Grange in Nottinghamshire, North Sea Camp in Lincolnshire and Hollesley Bay in Suffolk, which functioned as summer camps. Based on the growing awareness that a major effect of imprisonment is to institutionalise the prisoner, to render him incapable of functioning in everyday life and reinforce his criminality, a 'prison without walls', or open prison, as they have come to be called, was opened for adult prisoners in 1936 at New Hall Camp, near Wakefield. Today, 15 open prisons, many of which function as farms, have been established for prisoners who present no serious threat to public safety.

Sir Lionel Fox

The last of the prison commissioners to influence penal practice significantly was Sir Lionel Fox, Head of the Prison Commission between 1942 and 1960. Fox's legacy was to bring a more rigorous and scientific approach to the development of penal policy. As a reaction to public concern over increasing levels of crime, Fox commissioned research which sought to understand the causes of crime and the most effective ways of treating it.

Fox's final contribution was to influence the preparation of a White Paper, *Penal Practice in a Changing Society* (1959) which sought to bring the prison system up-to-date with changing social circumstances. The White Paper noted:

> It is a disquieting feature of our society that in the years since the war, rising standards in material prosperity, education and social welfare have brought no decrease in the higher rate of crime reached during the war; on the contrary, crime has increased and is still increasing . . . Existing penal methods have of necessity been developed piecemeal and imperfectly in response to experience and to the pressures of current problems.

In order to stem the rise in crime new prisons were built and the effective treatment of the persistent offender and the combating of recidivism were prioritised as the most important challenges facing the prison system.

In 1963 the Prison Commission was abolished and management of the prison system came under the direct responsibility of the Home Office. The following year, in a new regulatory framework for the management of prisons, the Prison Department spelled out the purpose of providing training and treatment programmes in prisons as follows:

> The purpose of the training and treatment of convicted prisoners shall be to encourage and assist them to lead a good and useful life.

> Prison Rule 1, 1964

The first security crisis

The expectation that by opening new prisons and subjecting prisoners to rigorous treatment programmes the crime rate would be reduced proved short-lived. Towards the end of the 1960s, as the need to contain increasing numbers of prisoners and rising levels of industrial unrest amongst prison staff became the predominant issues for the Prison Department to resolve, support for training and treatment programmes was gradually replaced by a growing emphasis on containment and the need for tighter managerial efficiency.

Public concern over the increasing number of prison escapes—in 1946 there were 864 escapes and attempted escapes, in 1964 there were 2,090—reached a head with the high profile escape of two of the 'Great Train Robbers', Charles Wilson from Birmingham in 1964 and Ronald Biggs from Wormwood Scrubs in 1965, as well as the spy George Blake from Wormwood Scrubs in 1966.

35

The then home secretary, Roy Jenkins, responded to the furore which followed by appointing a Committee of Inquiry, under Lord Mountbatten of Burma, to investigate prison security and to make recommendations for improvement. The inquiry was significant because, although it did not completely discount the value of training and treatment programmes in prisons, it did raise concern that the liberalisation of prison regimes had been carried out at the expense of prison security.

The Mountbatten Report recommended that prisoners should be divided into four categories (A, B, C and D) according to their security risk, and that the highest risk prisoners should be kept in a new maximum security prison, which was to be specifically designed and built for the purpose on the Isle of Wight. The prison, to be called 'Vectis', would

> house those prisoners who must in no circumstances be allowed to get out, whether because of the security considerations affecting spies, or because their violent behaviour is such that members of the public or the police would be in danger of their lives if they were to get out.

While the proposals for security categories were adopted by the government—from this point on all prisons were to be designated according to the security category of the majority of prisoners held within them—the proposal for a single high security prison was rejected. Instead, the Advisory Council on the Penal System was asked by the government to re-consider the nature of the regime under which high security prisoners should be held.

The Advisory Council appointed a sub-committee, chaired by Sir Leon Radzinowicz, which in 1968 published a report, *The Regime for Long Term Prisoners in Conditions of Maximum Security*, which opposed the proposal that all high security prisoners should be held in one large gaol. The report argued that in such a prison

> There is a danger that the atmosphere might become repressive with the staff attitudes becoming affected by their anxieties about the attitudes and activities of a concentrated group of evil men who felt themselves finally rejected by society and who felt they had nothing to gain by co-operation and nothing to lose by revolt.

In its place, the committee proposed that high security prisoners should be dispersed amongst a small number of very secure prisons, to be upgraded for the purpose, known as dispersal prisons.

The change in attitude towards the purpose of imprisonment, which the escapes and the subsequent enquiries helped bring about, was articulated in the government White Paper, *People in Prison* (1969). Its conclusion that

neither our capacity for the diagnosis of the needs of offenders, nor the ability to effect a cure is as great as many advocates of this or that form of treatment have implied

marked the beginning of a period of more than two decades in which deterrence and containment replaced reformation and rehabilitation as the overriding aims of imprisonment.

The May Committee

During the 1970s industrial relations deteriorated in prisons as members of the principal trade union, the Prison Officers' Association (POA), engaged in various forms of industrial action.

In 1979, the *Committee of Inquiry into the United Kingdom Prison Services* was convened, under the chairmanship of Sir John May, to look into questions of pay, leave, hours of duty and the grading of prison staff. The May Committee concluded that staff had become disillusioned and sceptical about the treatment objectives of imprisonment, while at the same time it was concerned that increasing levels of security had limited their areas of responsibility.

Influenced to a great extent by the 'Nothing Works' research, carried out by Robert Martinson in 1974 (see *Chapters 1* and *6*), the May Committee argued that 'the rhetoric of treatment and training had had its day and should be replaced'. It proposed that a new concept— 'positive custody' should become the guiding principle of imprisonment. In practical terms this would have meant that the principal purpose of work, education, physical exercise and other activities, would no longer be to attempt to influence the behaviour of prisoners, but, more prosaically, it would be to keep them occupied and to maintain their physical and mental well-being.

The committee also made a number of recommendations which affected pay and other conditions of service for prison officers. However, staff unrest did not disappear overnight and disputes over shift allowances, overtime pay and manning levels were to remain unresolved for many years.

In 1987 a new set of working arrangements, known as 'Fresh Start', were introduced for prison officers. In effect, this was a pay and productivity deal which meant a reduction in the working week and an end to overtime. A lot, but far from all, of the power of the POA disappeared with the phasing out of overtime.

RECENT HISTORY

In 1988 Prison Rule No 1 (see page 35) was supplemented by a new 'Statement of Purpose' for the Prison Service in England and Wales which remains current. It reads:

> Her Majesty's Prison Service serves the public by keeping in custody those committed by the courts. Our duty is to look after them with humanity and help them lead law abiding lives in custody and after release.

The Strangeways riot

Prison riots are a relatively recent phenomenon in the history of the prison system in England and Wales. A famous riot took place at Dartmoor in 1932, but there was no major recurrence until 1969 when a riot at Parkhurst, then a top security prison on the Isle of Wight, resulted in serious injuries to both prisoners and staff. During the 1970s and 1980s however, riots became an increasingly prevalent feature of prison life.

Serious disturbances occurred in a number of prisons, including Gartree prison in Leicestershire, Hull and Wormwood Scrubs. In the 1980s, sit down protests spread to some lower security prisons and to local prisons. In April 1986 rioting erupted in over 40 prisons. Then on 1 April 1990, the largest and most prolonged riot in penal history occurred at Strangeways, a busy local prison in Manchester. During a period of 25 days, the public watched daily television pictures of prisoners hurling slates from prison roof tops, as the riot spread to more than 20 other prisons throughout the country. When the rioting finally subsided, tens of millions of pounds of public money were required to repair the damage caused to the prison estate.

The Woolf Report

The inquiry into the causes of the Strangeways and other riots proved to be the most wide ranging and thorough inquiry into the work and conditions of the prison system ever conducted. The report of the Inquiry, which was conducted by Lord Woolf and Sir Stephen Tumim, was published in February 1991. *Prison Disturbances April 1990: Report of an Inquiry,* was 600 pages long and contained 204 specific proposals and recommendations for the wholesale reform of the prison system.

The report exposed long standing problems within the prison system—overcrowding, poorly maintained prisons, bad management and a lack of justice and humanity towards prisoners. In particular, Woolf was scathing about the conditions under which remand prisoners were held. The number of remand prisoners had risen from an average of 6,438 in 1980 to 11,440 in 1988, an increase of 77 per cent. The Woolf

38

Inquiry reported that they were held in overcrowded conditions, confined to their cell for up to 22 hours per day and had few opportunities to engage in constructive activities.

In order to give the work of the Prison Service a clearer sense of direction, Lord Woolf proposed there should be a complete reassessment of the purpose of imprisonment. The central finding of the report—that stability in prisons depends on maintaining a balance between three basic principles: security, control and justice—was explained in the following terms:

> . . . "Security" refers to the obligations of the Prison Service to prevent prisoners escaping. "Control" deals with the obligation of the Prison Service to prevent prisoners being disruptive. "Justice" refers to the obligation of the Prison Service to treat prisoners with humanity and fairness, and to prepare them for their return to the community in a way which makes it less likely that they will re-offend.

Proposals for reform were distilled into 12 central recommendations. These were:

- Closer co-operation between the different parts of the criminal justice system. For this purpose a national forum and local committees should be established.

- More visible leadership of the Prison Service by the director general who is seen to be the operational head and in day-to-day charge of the service. To achieve this there should be a published 'compact' or 'contract' given by ministers to the director general of the Prison Service, who should be responsible for the performance of that contract and publicly answerable for the day to day operations of the Prison Service.

- Increased delegation of responsibility to governors of establishments.

- An enhanced role for prison officers.

- A 'compact' or 'contract' for each prisoner setting out the prisoner's expectations and responsibilities in the prison in which he or she is held.

- A national system of Accredited Standards with which, in time, each prison establishment would be required to comply.

- A new Prison Rule that no establishment should hold more prisoners than is provided for in its certified normal level of accommodation with provisions for Parliament to be informed if exceptionally there is to be a material departure from that rule.

- A public commitment from ministers setting a timetable to provide access to sanitation for all inmates at the earliest practicable date not later than February 1996.

- Better prospects for prisoners to maintain their links with families and the community through more visits and home leaves and through being located in community prisons as near to their homes as possible.

- A division of prison establishments into small and more manageable and secure units.

- A separate statement of purpose, separate conditions and generally a lower security categorisation for remand prisoners.

- Improved standards of justice within prisons involving the giving of reasons to a prisoner for any decision which materially and adversely affects him or her; a grievance procedure and disciplinary proceedings which ensure that the governor deals with most matters under his or her present powers; relieving Boards of Visitors of their adjudicatory role; and providing for final access to an independent Complaints Adjudicator.

The White Paper, *Custody, Care and Justice*

The Woolf Report was welcomed by many people who worked within the criminal justice system for its openness and breadth. The government responded in the same year by publishing a White Paper, *Custody, Care and Justice: The Way Ahead for the Prison Service in England and Wales*, which accepted all of the recommendations with the exception of one: that there should be a cap on prison overcrowding. The government also announced that no further resources would be made available to implement the recommendations and that they would be implemented over a period of 20-25 years.

Custody, Care and Justice summarised the priorities for the Prison Service as follows:

- To improve necessary security measures.

- To improve co-operation with other services and institutions, by working closely with the probation service and by membership of a national forum and area committees.

- To increase delegation of responsibility and accountability to all levels; with clear leadership and a published annual statement of objectives.

- To improve the quality of jobs for staff.

- To recognise the status and particular requirements of unconvicted prisoners.

- To provide active and relevant programmes for all prisoners, including unconvicted prisoners.

- To provide a code of standards for conditions and activities in prisons to be used to set improvement targets in the annual contracts made between prison governors and their area managers.

- To improve relationships with prisoners, including a statement of facilities for each prisoner, sentence plans, consultations, reasons for decisions and access to an independent appeal body for grievances and disciplinary decisions.

- To provide access to sanitation at all times for all prisoners.

- To end overcrowding.

- To divide the larger wings in prisons into smaller, more manageable units wherever possible.

A previous White Paper, *Crime, Justice and Protecting the Public* (1990), had outlined the new thinking regarding the function of imprisonment:

> It was once believed that prison, properly used, could encourage a high proportion of offenders to start an honest life on their release. Nobody now regards imprisonment, in itself, as an effective means of reform for most prisoners . However much prison staff try to inject a positive purpose into the regime, as they do, prison is a society which requires no sense of personal responsibility from prisoners. Normal social or working habits do not fit. The opportunity to learn from other criminals is pervasive. For most offenders, imprisonment has to be justified in terms of public protection, denunciation and retribution. Otherwise it can be an expensive way of making bad people worse. The prospects for reforming offenders are usually much better if they stay in the community, provided the public is properly protected.

41

Furthermore, *Crime, Justice and Protecting the Public* questioned whether it was realistic to expect that longer and more frequent prison sentences deterred potential offenders from committing crimes:

Deterrence is a principle with much immediate appeal. Most law abiding citizens understand the reasons why some behaviour is made a criminal offence, and would be deterred by the shame of a criminal conviction or the possibility of a severe penalty. There are doubtless some criminals who carefully calculate the possible gains and risks. But much crime is committed on impulse, given the opportunity presented by an open window or unlocked door, and is committed by offenders who live from moment to moment; their crimes are as impulsive as the rest of their feckless, sad or pathetic lives. It is unrealistic to construct sentencing arrangements on the assumption that most offenders will weigh up the possibilities in advance and base their conduct on rational calculation. Often they do not.

The Criminal Justice Act 1991
The Criminal Justice Act 1991 encouraged sentencers to divert less serious offenders away from custody, but simultaneously to treat violent and sexual offenders more harshly. As a result, the number of custodial sentences dropped dramatically and the prison population began to decline for the first time since the Second World War. In fact, the decline actually began before the Act was passed as sentencers reacted to the change in thinking and as a result of the training they were receiving on its contents.

As well as introducing a new range of community based penalties for less serious offenders, the Act also contained important changes to the calculation and meaning of sentences, and to release mechanisms.

Under the Act, all prisoners serving up to four years are released automatically at the half-way point. Those serving up to 12 months are not supervised, but all prisoners with sentences of 12 months and longer are supervised by the Probation Service.

Prisoners with a sentence of four years or more are eligible for release on parole between the half way point and the two thirds point of their sentence. Separate arrangements apply to lifers (see *Chapter 4*).

The Criminal Justice Act 1991 also established a framework for the contracting out of prison escort services and the running of certain prisons by the private sector. In 1991, nine companies tendered for the management of the first privately run prison, the Wolds Remand Centre, on Humberside. The contract was awarded to Group 4 Security Services and the Wolds opened in 1992, since when six more prisons have been contracted out to private sector management with more to come (see *Chapter 3*).

42

The Prison Service becomes a Next Steps agency of government

In 1992, a review of the overall management structure of the Prison Service was carried out by Admiral Sir Raymond Lygo. Lygo recommended that the Prison Service should become a 'Next Steps' agency of government, headed by a new director general to be chosen by open competition. He argued that the development of Prison Service policy should continue to rest with government while responsibility for day-to-day operational matters should rest with the Prison Service. Lygo argued that this greater autonomy would ensure improved efficiency and unity of purpose within the Prison Service.

The Prison Service achieved 'agency status' in April 1993. At the same time, Derek Lewis became the first director general to be appointed from a private sector commercial background. He had no previous experience of the prison system.

'Prison works'

By the beginning of 1993, the government had begun to grow embarrassed by the Woolf Report and its own White Paper. A new uncompromising approach to law and order and a belief in the effectiveness of imprisonment to reduce crime became the order of the day. Michael Howard, home secretary between May 1993 and May 1997, set out the new approach at the Conservative Party Conference on 6 October 1993 when he declared: 'Let us be clear: prison works'. Announcing a package of 27 measures, Mr Howard admitted that

> This may mean that more people will go to prison. I do not flinch from that. We shall no longer judge the success of our system of justice by a fall in the prison population.

To support the new approach, Michael Howard invoked the symbolic purpose of imprisonment—that it was the response to crime demanded by victims in the interests of retribution. He also stressed two of the three major utilitarian purposes—prison incapacitated and it deterred offenders from committing further crimes: 'It [prison] ensures that we are protected from murderers, muggers and rapists, and it makes many who are tempted to commit crime think twice'. No mention was made of the purpose of imprisonment to rehabilitate offenders.

Furthermore, in an attempt to increase the deterrent quotient of imprisonment, Michael Howard announced that prison conditions should be made 'decent, but austere'. Although few practical changes resulted from this commitment to austerity, reform of the kind promoted by Woolf returned to the back burner.

43

The second security crisis

As was the case in the 1960s, the escape of high security prisoners in 1994 and 1995 caused serious questions to be asked about the ability of the prison system to protect the public from dangerous offenders. Although the escape of six high security prisoners from Whitemoor prison in Cambridgeshire in 1994 and three from Parkhurst on the Isle of Wight in early 1995 occurred at a time when the overall number of escapes was declining and all nine were caught within a short period of time, the official inquiries which followed have had major implications for the work of the Prison Service ever since.

The Woodcock Report which described events leading to the escape of six prisoners from the Special Secure Unit (see *Chapter 3*) at Whitemoor prison, five of whom were IRA terrorists, and the subsequent discovery of about one pound of Semtex explosive within the perimeter walls, criticised prison officers at the prison for not carrying out the most basic security procedures. The inquiry found that prisoners had fooled and intimidated staff into believing that they could not and would not escape. Serious inadequacies in the way the prison was managed were exposed. Warnings that prisoners were enjoying too much freedom had not been heeded and previous recommendations for improving security procedures had not been acted upon. In conclusion, Sir John Woodcock, who carried out the inquiry, described the escape as

a disaster waiting to happened . . . At times it was difficult to find something being done in accordance with the manuals . . . it appears that everything which could have gone wrong has in fact done so . . . so many things were wrong, so many procedures and policies totally ignored and with such regularity that the escape could have taken place on any day of the week with the same chance of success.

In order to avoid further disasters, the Woodcock Report recommended the introduction of controls on the amount of property prisoners could keep in their cells, more frequent searching of prisoners, visitors and staff, and an increased use of dog patrols and CCTV.

The report which described the escapes from Parkhurst prison proved to be even more damning. The inquiry, carried out by General Sir John Learmont, included a comprehensive review of security in other high security prisons throughout England and Wales. It found that

Whitemoor and Parkhurst were not aberrations of the norm but symptomatic of the practices in place in similar establishments throughout the country.

Overall, the impression left by the inquiry was that the prison system was under unremitting pressure and that prison staff were demoralised and in need of strong and direct leadership. The report was particularly scathing about the quality of management, both at Parkhurst and, more significantly, at headquarters: 'Positive and visible leadership at all levels is required to move the service forward'. The inquiry identified two particular areas of concern. First, there are elements within the fundamental management philosophy and practice which appeared wholly inappropriate and, second, there were severe problems within the management structure of the service.

The Woodcock and Learmont reports have been strongly criticised by prison reformers but most of their recommendations have been acted upon. One which has not is the recommendation in the Learmont report that all top security prisoners should be contained in one maximum security prison.

Publication of the Learmont report led the then home secretary, Michael Howard, to respond to the criticisms of management it contained by sacking the director general of the Prison Service, Derek Lewis. This provoked a very fierce and public debate about who was ultimately accountable for the prison system—the Home Office or the Prison Service or both. In 1996, Derek Lewis successfully won £280,000 from the Home Office in compensation for unfair dismissal.

The Crime (Sentences) Act 1997
The Conservative government pursued policies designed to increase the prison population right up until it lost the general election in May 1997. The 1997 Act sought to reduce the discretion of sentencers by introducing mandatory prison sentences of seven years for third time drug suppliers, three years for third time domestic burglars, and a mandatory life sentence for second time serious sexual or violent offenders. It also introduced the concept of 'honesty in sentencing', which would have required all offenders to serve a minimum of 85 per cent of the sentence handed down by the court in prison, thereby abolishing the system of automatic release introduced by the Criminal Justice Act 1991.

To date, the Labour government has enacted only those provisions of the Act which are unlikely to increase the prison population to any great extent. Most significantly, mandatory minimum sentences for third time burglars have not been implemented because of the current pressures on prison capacity. 'Honesty in sentencing' (which, in practice, would have proved far from honest) has been abandoned totally.

45

CHAPTER 3

Prisons

THE PRISON ESTATE

No two prisons are the same. The prison estate in England and Wales is comprised of 139 separate prison establishments, all of which vary considerably in terms of size, date of construction, design, level of physical security and status—i.e. whether they hold remand prisoners, women prisoners, young offenders etc.

Some prisons accommodate fewer than 100 prisoners, others cater for over 1,000. Some prisons date back to the last century or before and were inherited by the state when it took over the management of the prison system in 1877. There are 44 prisons which contain listed buildings and five with scheduled ancient monuments. For example, Lancaster prison is a medieval castle keep. Dover and the Verne are nineteenth century forts. Reading Remand Centre is built on the site of a medieval monastery.

There are prisons which were once army camps or country houses, while others have been purpose built. Some prisons are situated in rural areas and contain large open spaces, others—particularly prisons built before 1900—are situated in densely populated urban areas and suffer from cramped conditions. Depending on the type and age of the prison, the living accommodation varies from individual cells to dormitories.

Broadly speaking, prisons are divided into local prisons, which accommodate unconvicted prisoners on remand and those serving short sentences, and training prisons, which accommodate all other sentenced prisoners. Training prisons are sub-divided according to the type and security category of the prisoners contained within them. For instance, high security prisoners are held in dispersal prisons, while young offenders under the age of 21 are held in young offender institutions (YOIs).

In addition, there are a small number of specialist prisons which have been designed for particular groups of prisoners. These include one High Intensity Training Centre, or 'boot camp' as it is popularly known, for young offenders; three resettlement prisons for long term prisoners nearing release; a prison which provides a therapeutic regime designed to change the behaviour of serious violent and sexual offenders; and an industrial prison where prisoners work in industrial workshops for above average wages. There are also seven prisons which have been contracted out of the public sector and are managed by private companies.

A recent addition to the prison estate is a prison ship, HMP Weare, which was purchased from America in 1997 to ease prison overcrowding and is now moored off the coast at Portland, Dorset.

Around two thirds of the 139 prisons in England and Wales are closed training prisons or local prisons. All 139 prisons are categorised as follows:

	No	Per cent
Local prisons (male)	34	25
Closed training prisons (male)	58	43
Open training prisons (male)	12	9
Remand centres	17	13
Closed YOIs (male)	18	13
Open YOIs (male)	4	3
Closed YOIs (female)	2	1
Local prisons (female)	5	4
Closed training prisons (female)	6	4
Open training prisons (female)	3	2
Private prisons	7	4

PRISON DESIGN

During the late eighteenth and nineteenth centuries, prison design was guided by the need to accommodate large numbers of prisoners and to ensure ease of supervision by a minimum number of staff. To this end, the philosopher, Jeremy Bentham, developed the so-called Panopticon, or 'all seeing' prison. The Panopticon was never built. But the basic principle of a radial design remained the standard until a 'new wave' of prison building commenced in the early 1960s.

The radial design is comprised of wings which radiate from a central atrium so that the whole prison can be monitored by one officer standing at the hub. Pentonville prison in London exemplified the design. It was built in 1842 to contain up to 520 prisoners who slept, worked and ate in individual cells, monitored by only 20 guards. The design was so admired that 54 copies of Pentonville were built between 1843 and 1850. Today, although ideas about prison design have been updated, it is the Victorian built prisons, such as Pentonville, Winson Green, Armley and Durham which remain the backbone of the prison system.

47

Between 1918 and 1958, no new purpose built prisons were opened. Since 1958 the prison building programme has included new design high security prisons and young offender institutions. Thirty new prisons were added to the estate during the 1960s and 1970s and between 1980 and the present day a further 30 prisons have been added. The present building programme involves the construction of six new prisons before the end of the century.

During the 1960s and 1970s so called 'hotel corridor' style prisons were built with cells arranged along short stud corridors with dead ends. Each corridor was built to contain about 75 prisoners, so creating a much more personal environment than that afforded by the radial design. Cell blocks were built around communal areas and these, along with educational facilities, workshops and playing fields were all contained within a secure perimeter. Blundeston prison in Suffolk typified the design and was much copied.

More recently, new design, or 'new generation' prisons, as they are called in America where they originate, have been designed according to new concepts of security. They are comprised of separate three-sided units containing small groups of prisoners, the cells being wrapped around a central association space. Each unit is managed by a multi-disciplinary team, charged with developing regime activities which respond to the particular needs of the prisoners under their control. Examples of 'new generation' prisons include Woodhill in Milton Keynes, Lancaster Farms and Doncaster.

PRISON SECURITY

It is a primary duty of the Prison Service to maintain standards of security and control in prisons. Security means preventing prisoners escaping, either from prison or while under escort outside of prison. Control means maintaining order in prison. As a loss of control can result in a breach of security, the way that prisons are designed and governed is central to ensuring that prisoners are held securely.

As we saw in *Chapter 2*, since the late 1960s all prisons and prisoners have been categorised according to a security system proposed by the inquiry into prison security, carried out by Lord Mountbatten of Burma. This recommended that all prisoners should be divided into four categories, according to the level of security required for their safe containment and control. Today, prisoners are classified according to

their age, temperament and record and with a view to maintaining good order and facilitating training and, in the case of convicted prisoners, of furthering the purpose of their training and treatment.

The four security categories are A, B, C, and D, with A representing the highest category. All categorisation of prisoners is subject to review, so enabling individuals to be moved up or down the scale.

- *Category A* prisoners are those 'whose escape would be highly dangerous to the public or the police or the security of the state, no matter how unlikely that escape might be; and for whom the aim must be to make escape impossible'.

- *Category B* prisoners are those 'for whom the very highest conditions of security are not necessary but for whom escape must be made very difficult'.

- *Category C* prisoners are those 'who cannot be trusted in open conditions but who do not have the resources and will to make a determined escape attempt'.

- *Category D* prisoners are those 'who can reasonably be trusted in open conditions.

The Prison Service allocates prisoners according to an assessment of their security risk. Prisoners convicted of serious offences, such as murder or rape are likely to be given a security category of A and be held in dispersal prisons; category B prisoners are held either in dispersal prisons or category B closed training prisons; category C prisoners are held in closed training prisons that have lower perimeter security; and category D prisoners are held in open training prisons, where there are few physical barriers to escape.

Remand prisoners are held in local prisons, all of which are category B. Young offenders between the ages of 15-21 are held in young offender institutions, although increasing numbers are currently held in adult prisons, due to the pressures of overcrowding. Women are held in separate all-female prisons, or in separate all-female wings within male prisons.

Levels of physical security are highest in dispersal and category B prisons, where perimeter security includes the use of various electronic security systems, such as CCTV and 'geophone' alarm systems. The perimeter of prisons holding category A and B prisoners consists of an internal fence or fences made of closely-meshed wire topped with barbed tape, and an external wall topped with an anti-climbing device. The empty space between the outermost fence and the wall is designated a sterile area and is kept out of bounds to both prisoners and staff. Perimeter security in category C prisons normally consists of a perimeter wall or fence topped with barbed tape only. Open prisons do not normally maintain a secure perimeter of any kind. The boundary of open prisons may be marked with a small fence. Security and control is maintained through a mixture of low levels of physical security and the development of regimes which aim to keep prisoners occupied in so called 'purposeful' activities.

LOCAL PRISONS AND REMAND CENTRES

Unconvicted prisoners are remanded to custody in local prisons, so called because they accommodate prisoners awaiting trial in local courts. They also accommodate prisoners awaiting sentence, sentenced prisoners awaiting allocation to training prisons and prisoners serving very short sentences, including fine defaulters and civil prisoners.

As far as possible, unconvicted prisoners are kept apart from convicted prisoners and are subject to a separate set of rules, designed to accord with their legal status of 'innocent unless and until proved guilty'.

The majority of young offenders on remand are held in separate remand centres, although overcrowding in recent years has meant that an increasing number are held in adult local prisons.

The Prison Service Statement of Purpose for unconvicted prisoners states the following:

> Unconvicted prisoners are presumed to be innocent. Subject to the duty to hold them and deliver them to court securely and to the need to maintain order in establishments they will be treated accordingly and, in particular, will be allowed all reasonable facilities to seek release on bail; preserve their accommodation and employment; prepare for trial; maintain contact with relatives and friends; pursue legitimate business and social interests; [and] obtain help with personal problems.

Local prisons tend to be situated in densely populated urban areas in close proximity to the courts which they serve. The majority date from Victorian times and are characterised by old and inadequate buildings.

Overcrowding is also a problem because local prisons are constrained from transferring prisoners to other prisons by the need to hold remand prisoners within a close distance of the courts at which their cases are to be heard. Problems are compounded by poor quality regimes, a consequence of the limited facilities available for work, education and training in local prisons.

Although the p rison building programme has provided 12 new prisons for unconvicted prisoners since 1980 and money has been provided to improve the existing estate, many local prisons remain in poor condition and continue to suffer from the effects of severe overcrowding.

DISPERSAL PRISONS

Dispersal prisons are top-security prisons where category A prisoners are held. With the exception of Wakefield, they are all relatively new and so offer some of the best physical conditions within the prison system. At present there are five dispersal prisons: Frankland, Full Sutton, Long Lartin, Wakefield and Whitemoor. Another prison, Belmarsh, although not officially designated as a dispersal prison is managed as one because it accommodates a small number of high security prisoners in a Special Secure Unit (see below) and it functions as the most secure remand prison in London.

As we saw in *Chapter 2*, there are strong arguments over whether category A prisoners should be concentrated in one high security prison, or dispersed throughout a number of higher security prisons. The Radzinowicz Committee (1968) acknowledged that 'neither solution is a panacea'. It suggested that one high security prison could be perceived by prisoners as a place of last resort, thereby provoking high levels of frustration and violence, and that the demands on staff would be considerable.

The theory of dispersal suggests that it is both safer and more humane to accommodate high security prisoners amongst a larger group of prisoners, who pose less threat to society and are less likely to present a serious control problem or riot. On the other hand, the dispersal system is expensive and imposes an unwarranted degree of security on category B prisoners held in the same establishment.

Special secure units
The dispersal system has been reviewed consistently since it was introduced. The May Committee of 1979 decided in favour of maintaining the dispersal system while, at the same time, acknowledging its difficulties. The Control Review Committee of 1984 endorsed the May Committee's scepticism and recommended that security should be upgraded in all dispersal prisons and that a small number of special units for prisoners who present control problems should be established. A helicopter-assisted escape from Gartree prison in 1987 led to a further review which sub-classified category A prisoners according to whether they were an exceptional risk, high risk or standard risk. Exceptional risk prisoners are now kept in special secure units (SSUs).

51

Basically, prisons within a prison, SSUs accommodate a small number of prisoners who pose an exceptional security risk, such as terrorists, large scale drug importers and prisoners who repeatedly attempt to escape. Such prisoners are kept separately from other prisoners and are subject to separate regimes. All prisoners in SSUs are subject to closed visits, during which they are separated from their visitors by a glass screen.

SSUs are the most expensive category of prison accommodation to run. The average cost per prisoner place is approximately £61,000 per annum. Dispersal prisons, the next most expensive category of prison accommodation, have an operating cost per prisoner place of £33,000 per annum.

Super-maximum security prisons

As we saw in *Chapter 2*, the 1995 Learmont Report recommended the establishment of a high security prison for top security prisoners. Learmont also wanted one for particularly disruptive prisoners. He was undoubtedly influenced by the introduction of high security prisons, known as 'Super-max' prisons, in America, where they are now firmly embedded into standard correctional practice. Particular prisons, such as Florence in Colorado and Pelican Bay in California have received considerable attention worldwide. Much of this has been highly critical of the way that prisoners are isolated in separate windowless cells and the extremely limited educational and exercise activities.

In this country, an inquiry carried out by the government's former chief medical officer, Sir Donald Acheson, found that prisoners who are isolated for long periods in SSUs and who have only limited opportunities to associate with other prisoners and staff, may suffer a deterioration in their mental health. The report of the inquiry, completed in 1996, has not been published. It recommended that prisoners should be held in SSUs for as short a period as possible; that more opportunities for mental stimulation and physical exercise should be provided; and that prisoners should have access to open visits with members of their immediate family. It concluded that

> the combination of uncertainty concerning the sentence plan and the length of stay on the unit, together with lack of opportunities for meaningful work, natural visual and auditory stimuli, social contact outside a small group of prisoners, incentives, and physical contact with families and friends, if sustained for several years is likely to lead to significant adverse effects on mental health in a proportion of prisoners.

At present, the claustrophobic environment within SSUs means that prisoners are subject to frequent health checks. This was a factor which may have influenced the former chief inspector of prisons, Sir Stephen Tumim, to describe Learmont's recommendation for the establishment of a high security fortress prison as 'the road to the concentration camp'.

YOUNG OFFENDER INSTITUTIONS (YOIs)

Prior to 1982, there were a number of different options open to the courts for the sentencing of offenders under the age of 21. Boys over the age of 14 who were sentenced to custody in a detention centre had to conform to the requirements of a regime based on military style corrective training, the aim of which was to instil a sense of discipline in young offenders. The regime consisted of hard physical work and strenuous physical exercise and required all offenders to maintain extremely high standards of order and cleanliness. Lasting for between three and six months, the underlying theory behind the sentence was that by imposing discipline on offenders, they would eventually impose it on themselves.

During the 1950s and 1960s, the military rigour of detention centres was modified. However, it came back with a vengeance in the early 1980s when four experimental 'short, sharp, shock' regimes were piloted. It proved to be a spectacular failure. An evaluation carried out by the Home Office in 1984 reported that

> The introduction of the pilot project regimes had no discernible effect on the rate at which trainees are re-convicted.

The report concluded that instead of reducing the likelihood of offending, regimes which emphasise high levels of physical work and training are positively welcomed by young offenders. They tend to appeal to their macho self-image and produce ex-prisoners who are more criminally sophisticated and physically capable of committing crimes such as burglary.

The other main option pre-1982—borstal training—attempted to turn young offenders away from crime by instilling in them notions of good citizenship. The borstal vision had also corrupted over the years, and by the 1970s they were generally considered to be outmoded.

The Criminal Justice Act 1982 created a new sentencing structure for young offenders. This extended the range of community sanctions, introduced new powers for imposing custodial sentences and abolished borstals, which became youth custody centres. Six years later, the Criminal Justice Act 1988 replaced detention centres and youth custody orders with a single custodial sentence for young offenders called 'detention in a young offender institution'. Today, young offenders, like adult offenders, are subject to determinate sentences of imprisonment.

There are 26 YOIs in England and Wales, three of which hold young female offenders. They accommodate offenders aged 15 to 20 inclusive (16-20 for girls). Many YOIs were originally built and opened as borstals, although the increase in the young offender population since 1990 has necessitated the building of three new purpose built YOIs.

YOIs are guided by Rule 3 of the Young Offender Institution Rules 1988, which states as follows:

> The aim of a young offender institution shall be to help offenders to prepare for their return to the outside community.
> The aim . . . shall be achieved, in particular, by:
> — providing a programme of activities, including education, training and work designed to assist offenders to acquire or develop personal responsibility, self-discipline, physical fitness, interests and skills, and to obtain suitable employment after release;
> — fostering links between the offender and the community;
> — cooperating with the services responsible for the offender's supervision after release.

Despite the emphasis placed in the rules on preparing young offenders for their return to the outside community, YOIs have been conspicuously unsuccessful in preventing young offenders from returning to a life of crime after their release. The latest Home Office figures show that 72 per cent of young offenders are re-convicted within two years of their release.

Recent reports produced by HM Chief Inspector of Prisons, which have described high levels of bullying, drug taking and idleness in some YOIs, have also raised concerns about the quality of regimes currently on offer. For example, Dover YOI was described in March 1997 as a

> veritable jungle, in which the strong preyed on the weak, and where most who entered the establishment had to physically fight to survive or exist as a vulnerable prisoner, subjected to continual intimidation and insult.

Summing up, the chief inspector wrote:

> Apart from offending the most basic standards of a civilised society these conditions are storing up increasing problems for the wider community. If you believe, as I do, that the way offenders are treated (i.e. firmly but fairly) influences their own future behaviour once they are released, then the forecast for society once many of these young men are released is not encouraging.

High Intensity Training Centres ('Boot camps')

A recent development for young offenders has been High Intensity Training Centres at Thorn Cross YOI and the use of Colchester Military Corrective Training Centre for a like purpose. More commonly known as 'boot camps', in many respects, the development of high intensity training appeared to signal a return to the 'short, sharp, shock' methods employed in detention centres in the early 1980s. However, in practice, the Colchester regime lasted only a year before closure, while Thorn Cross combines a very active regime with excellent throughcare arrangements.

Boot camps derive from courses of survival training provided for American military personnel during the Second World War. There are currently about 50 boot camps in 34 states throughout America. Regimes consist of a mixture of education, long hours of physical work and training and military style drill.

The decision to introduce boot camps in this country was made despite an extremely critical evaluation of US boot camps prepared by a team of high ranking Prison Service officials. The report, *Boot Camps, Report of a Visit to the United States, May 1994*, concluded:

> Nothing we saw, whilst we were in the US, either in the establishments we visited or in the research we have read, leads us to believe that boot camps appear to be any more effective than traditional prison in preventing future crimes.

Despite the negative findings, government ministers decided to pilot the two high intensity regimes for 'low risk' offenders between the ages of 17 and 21.

SECURE ACCOMMODATION FOR CHILDREN

Children under the age of 14, who have been sentenced under the Children and Young Persons Act 1933, are sent to various forms of secure accommodation which are managed by local authorities. Secure accommodation is also provided for 'juvenile' offenders with a history of absconding, or who are thought likely to abscond or injure themselves or others if placed in any other type of local authority accommodation. According to the Department of Health, there are currently 33 secure units in England and Wales which can hold up to 246 children at any one time. In addition, a small number of youth treatment centres accommodate children who are considered to be too dangerous for secure units.

An increase in the numbers of children who have been sentenced to custody by the courts has meant there is now an inadequate supply of places in secure units. An increasing number of older children are having to be held in YOIs, or adult prisons. In 1989, Judge Stephen Tumim, the then chief inspector of prisons, wrote:

> . . . Probably the most disturbing aspect to emerge from our inspections was the number of juveniles who continue to be held in penal establishments . . . In many ways, these youngsters have less in common with young men in their late teens than is generally realised. They are often despised by the older group, resented for their childishness and become victims of intimidation. Their presence can also have an adverse affect on the mature 17-20 age group. For instance, at Feltham, juveniles took up many of the resources in education at the expense of the education programme for other youngsters on remand . . .

In 1997, the present chief inspector, Sir David Ramsbotham, raised similar concerns in a thematic study of young offenders in prison, *Young Prisoners: A Thematic Review by HM Chief Inspector of Prisons for England and Wales* (1997):

> Many children and young adults are held in separate wings of adult local prisons. In some cases they share the same living accommodation as adult prisoners. Conditions for and treatment of young prisoners in local prisons vary enormously, as they do in young offender institutions. At the time of this review children and young adults were held in no fewer than 41 different Prison Service establishments.

Secure training centres (STCs)

So called persistent juvenile offenders have received an increasing amount of attention in recent years. A few have even achieved national notoriety by being given nicknames such as 'Rat Boy', 'Spider Boy' and 'Safari Boy' in the popular press. Notwithstanding the recent government decision to introduce secure training centres—prisons for 12 to 14 year olds, the question over whether such young criminals are in need of care or deserving of punishment has never been answered satisfactorily.

The first STC opened at Medway in Kent on 14 April 1998. Children between the ages of 12-14 may be sentenced to custody in a STC if they have been convicted of three or more imprisonable offences and they have re-offended during, or been in breach of, a supervision order. Sentences range between six months and two years, half of which is spent in custody and half in the community under the supervision of the Probation Service. The proposal is that five STCs will eventually hold 40 children each and be managed by private sector contractors. Medway STC is managed by Group 4.

Unsurprisingly, the introduction of STCs has proved controversial. Critics have argued that closed institutions are inappropriate for young children. They will foster further offending and bullying and self-harm will be common. It has also been suggested that they are not subject to child protection legislation and are in breach of the UN Convention on the Rights of the Child, which requires that the custody of juveniles is used only for the shortest time necessary. As such, they will be poorly regulated. Finally, they are expensive. It is estimated that STCs will cost up to £250,000 a year per child, money that would be better spent on enhancing community sanctions.

The government has attempted to counter such arguments by pointing to the quality of regime that will be available in STCs. It will emphasise education, sports and activities to improve social skills and self-esteem and each prisoner will have a member of staff as a personal mentor.

The government also appears to be persuaded by the potential of STCs to incapacitate persistent juvenile offenders. It has been asserted by the home secretary, Jack Straw that because the police, courts and social services have been unable to find ways to deal with juvenile offenders effectively in the past, at present there is no viable alternative to locking them up. Pursuant to the Crime and Disorder Act 1998, the government intends to introduce a new detention and training order, which will give the courts even greater powers to sentence 12 to 14 year olds to custody.

WOMEN'S PRISONS

At present, there are 16 prisons which accommodate women prisoners. Eleven accommodate women only and five accommodate both women and men in separate buildings or wings within buildings. All prisons shared by men and women have separate sleeping and living areas and male and female prisoners use separate workshops, class rooms, chapels, visiting rooms etc.

Holloway prison in London is the largest women's prison in western Europe. The remainder of the estate includes prisons which were previously closed male training prisons, remand centres or borstals. Due to the pressures of overcrowding in women's prisons, 1,000 extra places are to be created by extending the capacity in existing prisons and converting two male prisons for female use. Two new prisons are also planned—the first time that prisons, apart from

Holloway, will have been purpose-built specifically for women prisoners.

The small number of sentenced female prisoners who are regarded as dangerous or likely to attempt to escape are held in Durham prison, a high security local prison for male prisoners. A recent thematic review of women prisoners carried out by HM Chief Inspector of Prisons found that only about 30 per cent of women prisoners needed to be held in closed prisons because they posed a security risk. Notwithstanding, there are only three open prisons for women.

Despite not posing a serious risk to security and control, security for women prisoners has increased in recent years. Following the Woodcock and Learmont reports—both of which investigated prison security in response to the escape of men—security has been stepped up in female prisons much to the same extent as in male prisons. For example, opportunities for women prisoners to take temporary release have been reduced making it increasingly difficult for women to maintain contacts with their children or to find jobs.

Women are more likely than men to be imprisoned far from their homes, making visits from family and friends more difficult. Problems for women in maintaining family ties are exacerbated by the dominance of Holloway prison, which because of its size takes prisoners from all over the south of England.

Only four female prisons have mother and baby units, which provide facilities for mothers to keep their babies with them in prison. Many of the children of women prisoners have to be cared for by family or friends, or placed in the care of local authorities.

It is because the majority of prisoners are male that prisons for women tend to have developed as an afterthought. Prison rules and regulations, which have been designed to reflect the circumstances of male prisoners, have been applied retrospectively to women offenders. However, the background circumstances of women offenders—and especially the low risk to security that they present—suggests that the running of women's prisons should be treated as a distinct specialism. This was partially recognised finally in 1998, when an assistant director, supported by a Women's Policy Group, was appointed to develop model regimes for women prisoners.

OPEN PRISONS

Open prisons accommodate category D prisoners who are considered to present little or no danger to the general public should they escape. Such prisoners tend to include long term prisoners who have been gradually re-categorised to lower security categories as they near the

58

date of their release and prisoners who have committed non-violent crimes such as fraud. Open prisons have limited physical security and if prisoners abscond—the word used by the Prison Service to describe an escape from an open prison—they are re-categorised to 'C' or 'B' and transferred to closed prison conditions once they are recaptured.

Open prisons tend to be situated in rural areas and do not have perimeter walls around them. Accommodation is mostly in the form of dormitories, and large areas within the prison are devoted to open air activities such as market gardening and horticulture.

Open prisons do a good and useful job. But the lack of physical security is criticised regularly in the tabloid press which describes them as holiday camps. Stories suggesting that drink, drugs and sex are all freely available are common.

The situation has perhaps not been helped by the absence of a clear statement which describes the function of open prisons. An internal review of open prisons, published in 1996, recognised as much when it found that, although the first open prison was introduced into the prison system as long ago as 1933:

> We can draw little from history except that we have never purpose-built one single open prison. Nor, other than for economic reasons, do we have any philosophy for their being.

For the first time, the internal review attempted to produce a statement which clearly described the purpose of open prisons. It said that open prisons should provide an environment:

— in which prisoners begin to assume personal responsibility for their life in custody, with as much choice as possible within the constraints of the regime;
— where the range of activities and opportunities accord with those the prisoner would expect to meet in society and that the standards of performance expected of the prisoner are commensurate with those prevailing in society;
— in which the prisoner is given the opportunity to establish links with the community by a mixture of release into the community and the involvement of the community inside the prison;
— where the rules and regulations to run the prison community are kept to a minimum and are specific to open prisons rather than the residue of those applying to closed prisons.

Overall, the *Open Prisons Review* found that open prisons offer a 'cost effective use of resources' and that 'insufficient numbers of prisoners are currently benefiting from them'. It concluded that 'the Prison

Service agency should be less defensive about the role and purpose of open prisons'.

RESETTLEMENT PRISONS

Resettlement prisons form a small part of the prison estate to which selected prisoners are sent so that they can prepare for their release back into society. A relatively recent development, there are currently three resettlement prisons for adult male prisoners, the first of which opened in 1987. The three are: Latchmere House in Greater London, Blantyre House in Kent and Kirklevington Grange in Cleveland. Resettlement prisons differ from open prisons in that they take only prisoners approaching release, and who have been assessed as benefiting from the activities and opportunities provided by a resettlement regime.

The aim of resettlement regimes is to support prisoners to find paid work in the community, encourage them to obtain educational and vocational qualifications and address the personal and social factors which influenced them to offend.

In common with open prisons, little or no attempt has been made to evaluate their performance. Resettlement prisons have developed along different lines, influenced to a large extent by the vision and guidance of their respective governors. There is little co-ordination between resettlement prisons and no national forum in which to share and develop good practice.

However, despite a lack of official status within the Prison Service, resettlement prisons have achieved much in their short history. Although, as is the case in the open prison estate, security is based more on the development of good quality relationships between prisoners and staff than on high levels of physical security, fewer prisoners cause trouble and fewer abscond than prisoners in open prisons. More importantly, research completed by Brunel University shows that prisoners are nearly 50 per cent less likely to re-offend when released from Latchmere House resettlement prison than they are when released from other prisons.

OTHER SPECIALIST PRISONS

There are a small number of other specialist prisons within the prison system which aim to meet the needs of particular groups of prisoners. For example, Kingston Prison in Portsmouth specialises in holding older life sentence prisoners and Whatton Prison near Nottingham and Albany on the Isle of Wight specialise in the treatment of sex offenders.

Coldingley prison in Surrey is an 'industrial prison' which aims to employ prisoners in real life work situations. Prisoners work in large engineering workshops which produce various products for sale in the outside market.

Grendon prison near Aylesbury provides a therapeutic community for sexual and violent offenders. Prisoners selected for Grendon must agree to cooperate with the demands of the regime before they are transferred. The regime includes daily group meetings between prisoners and staff which aim to examine the offending behaviour of prisoners in the group. Although work and education are less important than in other prisons, institutional tasks such as cleaning and cooking take place alongside the therapeutic process.

Grendon has been the subject of a number of evaluation reports which have attempted to assess the relevance of therapeutic regimes to the Prison Service. The most recent report published by the Home Office found that 'lower rates of reconviction were found for prisoners who went to Grendon than for prisoners selected for Grendon but who did not go'. Moreover, 'for those who stayed at Grendon for longer periods, there appeared to be some reduction in reconviction rates for sexual and violent offences—particularly among sexual offenders'. A second therapeutic community regime is to be developed at a new private prison to open at Marchington in Staffordshire.

PRIVATELY MANAGED PRISONS

Private sector techniques—like the setting of performance targets—have been an increasing feature of the Prison Service in recent years, as they have of the public sector generally. During the 1980s, as part of its free market ideology, the Conservative government began selling off state-owned assets and transferring public services to the private sector. In 1984, the Adam Smith Institute, a right wing think-tank, published its *Omega Justice Policy*, which proposed that the government should privatise the building and running of prisons. It argued:

> Both security firms and hotel operations are commonplace in the private sector; it may be an oversimplification but a prison . . . involves little more than a combination of these two talents.

The argument received little support at the time. Even a majority of Conservative MPs considered that the privatisation of prisons was a privatisation too far.

Just over ten years ago, the principle that the state must take complete responsibility for administering punishment remained sacrosanct, as it had done since 1877 when the Prison Act brought all prisons under state control. As recently as 1987, in a speech to the House of Commons, the then home secretary, Douglas Hurd said

> I do not think there is a case, and I do not believe the House would accept a case, for auctioning or privatising the prisons or handing over the business of keeping prisoners safe to anyone other than government servants.

The turnaround in support for the privatisation of prisons that has occurred since has been remarkable. In 1988, the government published a Green Paper, *Private Involvement in the Remand Sector*, which proposed a limited privatisation experiment at new remand prisons. In 1991, the Lygo Report into prison management recommended that more prison services should be contracted out to the private sector, that the prison service should become an executive agency of government and that a far more commercial approach to the running of prisons should be adopted. A fundamental requirement of executive agencies is that they explore the 'market testing' of services, by inviting the private sector to compete against the state for contracts to deliver services (see Chapter 7).

The Criminal Justice Act 1991 gave the home secretary the power to 'contract-out' to the private sector the running of any prison, old or new, irrespective of status. Since then, the management of prisons, as well as the escorting of prisoners to courts, the delivery of prison education and a wide range of other services have been contracted out to the private sector.

A number of factors can be identified to explain why prison privatisation has made such headway.

First, the acceptance of privatisation is testament to the lobbying skills of a small number of pro-privatisation back bench Conservative MPs.

Second, privatisation provided the previous government with a useful stick with which to beat the Prison Officers Association, the union it considered was most responsible for blocking the development of its prison policies. Union opposition to prison privatisation has stemmed from the decision of private prisons not to employ ex-Prison Service officers and to deny the right of staff to join the POA.

Third, many senior civil servants and prison governors have been won over to privatisation by the opportunity it offers to try something new. Private prisons, it has been argued, could not be much worse than prisons presently run by the state.

Finally, as the privatisation of prisons has progressed, the Treasury has become increasingly attracted by the opportunity it presents of raising money on the commercial market to offset the high capital costs of building new prisons. Money to build the most recent private prisons has been secured through the Private Finance Initiative (PFI). Prisons funded through the PFI are built and financed by a private sector contractor, who is then paid by the Prison Service to manage the prison for a period of years specified in a contract.

The first contracts were for the management of prisons only. The first prison for over 100 years to be managed for private profit, the Wolds prison on Humberside, opened in 1992 as a local prison. It has since changed its status and now holds a mixture of remand and sentenced prisoners. The contract for the only existing prison to be market tested, Strangeways prison in Manchester, was won by the public sector after being re-built after the riot in 1990 (see *Chapter 2*). Blakenhurst prison, near Birmingham, along with Doncaster, was built originally for the Prison Service to manage, but was then later contracted out to the private sector before opening. The contract to manage Buckley Hall, near Rochdale, was won by the private sector, after a bid (allegedly, a cheaper one) was also lodged by the Prison Service.

The most recent private prisons—Altcourse in Liverpool, Parc in Bridgend and Lowdham Grange near Nottingham—have all been purpose built by the private sector. The contracts include the management, design, construction and finance (DCMF) of prisons.

In order to bid for contracts, companies interested in managing prisons had to show they had the experience and expertise necessary to meet the various responsibilities involved. To this end they formed joint ventures between management, construction and service companies. For example, the consortium which manages Doncaster prison, Premier Prisons Services Ltd., consists of Wackenhut, an American based security firm and Serco, a British facilities management company. Blakenhurst is managed by UK Detention Services Ltd., a joint venture between Corrections Corporation of America, the management company, and Sodexho, a French catering and facilities management corporation. The Wolds, Buckley Hall and Altcourse prisons are managed by Group 4 Prison Services Ltd, which previously had experience of managing Harmondsworth Immigration Detention Centre and later teamed up with Carter Goble Associates, an American planning and management consulting firm, and the British construction company Tarmac. Securicor Custodial Services Ltd, in order to support its bid for the DCMF contract to run Parc prison, formed a joint venture

63

with engineering company Atkins, architects Seifert and the construction company Costains.

A full list of private prisons currently in operation is as follows:

Opened	Status	Contractor	Contract
The Wolds, 1992	remand/ sentenced	Group 4	Managed
Blakenhurst, 1993	remand/ sentenced	UK Detention Services Ltd.	Managed
Doncaster, 1994	remand/ sentenced	Premier Prisons Services Ltd.	Managed
Buckley Hall, 1994	Cat C	Group 4	Managed
Altcourse, 1997	remand/ sentenced	Group 4	DCMF
Parc, 1997	remand/ sentenced	Securicor Custodial Services Ltd	DCMF
Lowdham Grange, 1998	Cat B	Premier Prison Services Ltd	DCMF

Privately managed prisons are run to specifications laid down in a contract between the Home Office and the company concerned. The full details of the contract are not published on the grounds of commercial confidentiality. Penalties may be imposed by the state if the terms of the contract are not met by the managing company. The enforcement of standards in this way is unique to the private sector and has been heralded by some commentators as a precursor to the establishment of enforceable minimum standards throughout the prison system as a whole. Both UK Detention Services and Securicor have been fined for failing to deal adequately with disturbances at Blakenhurst and Parc prisons respectively.

Instead of a governor, as in the public sector, each privately managed prison is managed by a 'director' who is an employee of the company. A 'controller', a Prison Service official, monitors the contract, reports to the home secretary on the running of the prison and carries out any adjudications. The home secretary has the power to install a state appointed governor if the director loses control of the running of the prison.

Private prisons are regulated by the Prison Rules, but the Prison Service Orders and Instructions need not apply (see *Chapter 7*). Prison rules apply in the same way in privately managed prisons as they do in publicly run prisons and prisoners retain the same legal rights. Prisoners use the same request and complaints system to pursue grievances and each prison is subject to inspection by HM Chief Inspector of Prisons and a Board of Visitors.

Arguments for and against private prisons

Proponents of privatisation argue that the involvement of the private sector has brought new ideas and new management techniques to the Prison Service and has acted as a spur to prisons in the public sector to develop new ways of working and deliver better value for money.

Another argument in favour of private prisons makes reference to research which has shown privately managed prisons to be between 8 to 15 per cent cheaper to run than 'like with like' comparitor prisons in the public sector.

Detractors argue that it should be the undiluted responsibility of the state to determine how prisons are run and that by delegating such responsibility to private companies, accountability for prison conditions and, it follows, the delivery of punishment, is in effect taken away from Parliament and placed in the hands of company share holders.

In addition, private prison contractors have a vested interest in a higher prison population. They form a powerful lobbying group, prepared, purely for business reasons, to argue for more frequent and longer sentences when there is a great deal of research which suggests the opposite—that the prison population should be reduced and more use be made of community sanctions.

Regarding the more practical matter of cost savings, doubt has been cast on the reliability of the Home Office research that has concluded privately managed prisons are more cost effective than those in the public sector. It has also been pointed out that, if privately managed prisons are cheaper to run, it is only because they employ fewer staff and offer less favourable pay and conditions of employment than do publicly run prisons. Staff at privately managed prisons receive lower salaries and pension contributions, are entitled to fewer holidays and in many cases are required to work a longer working week than their counterparts in the public sector.

Finally, the Prison Officers Association, along with some penal reform groups, have suggested that private prison contractors are lacking in experience and therefore naive when it comes to the day-to-day pressures and responsibilities associated with running prisons. All of the new private prisons have experienced serious incidents, including disturbances, high rates of bullying and suicides during the first 18 months after opening. Although this trend is not entirely unique to privately managed prisons, contractors have been criticised for admitting too many prisoners too quickly before staff have been able to grow accustomed to their roles and responsibilities.

The future of prison privatisation

In its response to a Home Affairs Committee report on *The Management of the Prison Service (Public and Private)*, December 1997, the new Labour government made clear it had changed its position on the future of prison privatisation. It said:

> While we accept that contracting out is not universally welcomed, we consider that the fears hitherto expressed over the principle of contracting out—that it would mean the abdication of state responsibility for public safety and the deprivation of freedom—have not proven justified, and that the idea of privately managed prisons is undoubtedly now more generally accepted, and should be allowed to develop further.

Further support for privatisation was signalled by the government when the home secretary, Jack Straw, publicly brushed aside his previous objections to privatisation by announcing to the POA National Conference in 1998 that 'the immediate transfer of existing private prisons to the public sector is not affordable and cannot be justified on value for money grounds'. For the foreseeable future all newly built prisons are likely to be funded through the PFI and managed by private interests.

However, it remains to be seen just how much of the criminal justice system will end up being privately run. In the meantime, there are a sufficient number of voices, ready to argue that the privatisation of prisons is both wrong in principle and flawed in practice. It would appear that the debate about the pros and cons of privatisation and the monitoring of the effectiveness of services is set to continue unabated.

CHAPTER 4

The Prison Population

Prison has often been described as a microcosm of society. Social critics and prison administrators have sometimes referred to the similarities between prisons and other institutions such as ships, hospitals, factories, hotels, monasteries, schools, small towns etc. But, although there are elements which prisons have in common with many social systems, in terms of the prison population—the offences committed, age, gender, ethnicity and social background etc.—there are fundamental differences between prisoners and the general population. There are also fundamental differences between prisoners themselves in terms of their status, the seriousness of the offences they have committed, the length of time they will remain in prison and the various ways in which they respond to the experience of imprisonment.

STATUS OF PRISONERS

As we have seen, prisons are used to hold people against their will for a number of different purposes. Apart from holding convicted prisoners, prisons are used to detain people awaiting trial, to enforce court orders and other punishments—for example if an offender fails to pay a fine or carry out a community sentence—and to hold asylum seekers or those threatened with deportation. In terms of the total prison population, those awaiting trial, those sent to prison for failure to meet court orders and those awaiting deportation, can often amount to around one-quarter.

In 1996, 43,000 prisoners (78 per cent) were serving sentences; about 11,600 prisoners (21 per cent) were on remand; and approximately 600 were non-criminal prisoners, including Immigration Act detainees and prisoners held for civil offences, such as contempt of court.

Gender, age and ethnicity
There are far more men than women in prison. In mid-1998, there was an average total prison population of 65,500. Of these, 52,500 were men and just 3,000 were women. Women prisoners form less than six per cent of the total prison population.

The prison population is much younger than the general population. More than half the prison population (56.5 per cent) is under 30. However, the number of older prisoners is beginning to rise. The number of prisoners aged 50 or over has increased by around 1,750 since 1990 and there was a total of 963 prisoners over the age of 60 at the end of October 1997.

People of ethnic minority origin are disproportionately represented within the prison population and there is also a growing proportion of foreign nationals. In 1996 there was an average of 10,200 people in prison known to be of ethnic minority origin—18 per cent of male prisoners and 24 per cent of female prisoners. In comparison, only about 5.5 per cent of the general population are from ethnic minorities. Over two-thirds of prisoners known to be of ethnic minority origin are African-Caribbean, compared to Asian prisoners who make up 16 per cent.

Social background
In 1991, the Home Office published a national survey of prisoners, which revealed that the socio-economic characteristics of the prison population differ from those of society as a whole in a number of important ways. The survey showed:

Family background
Prisoners are less likely to come from a stable family background than the general population. Approximately 26 per cent of prisoners had some experience of local authority care, compared with two per cent of the general population. Eight per cent of prisoners had spent most of their childhood in an institution. The proportion of prisoners coming from single parent households is higher than in the general population.

Marital status
Prisoners differ from the general population in terms of marital status. Nineteen per cent of prisoners were married prior to imprisonment, compared to 61 per cent of the general population. About 40 per cent of prisoners were single, nearly one third were cohabiting and 10 per cent were widowed. The longer that prisoners remain in prison, the more likely it is that they will become divorced or separated from their wives or partners.

Education
Prisoners leave school earlier, truant from school more frequently and have fewer educational qualifications than the general population. Forty three per cent of all prisoners said they left school before the age of 16

and a further 46 per cent said they left school at 16. Some 40 per cent of male prisoners under 25 said they left school prior to 16, compared to 11 per cent amongst the general male population.

Thirty per cent of prisoners said they mostly played truant from school after the age of 11, compared to three per cent of the general population.

Forty three per cent of prisoners had no qualifications when they went to prison. Over 45 per cent of the prison population under the age of 30 had no qualifications, compared with under 20 per cent of the general population. Thirty six per cent of prisoners had one or more GCSE O-levels as their highest qualification, eight per cent had an apprenticeship and a further eight per cent had some form of higher qualification.

Work experience

Prisoners are more likely to have experienced periods of unemployment than the general population. Prior to imprisonment about one third of prisoners were unemployed. A further seven per cent had an unofficial 'black economy' job or were living off crime. Six per cent of male prisoners and 12 per cent of females had never been in paid employment. A higher proportion of younger prisoners than older prisoners were unemployed prior to imprisonment. Forty per cent of prisoners under the age of 25 were unemployed, compared with 22 per cent of prisoners in their 40s and 50s. In 1991, fewer than 15 per cent of people under 25 in the general population were unemployed.

Prisoners who were employed prior to imprisonment had mostly been employed in unskilled and partly skilled occupations. Forty one per cent of male prisoners came from unskilled or partly skilled occupations, compared to 18 per cent of the general male population. Seventeen per cent of prisoners came from professional, intermediate and skilled non-manual professions, compared to 45 per cent of the general male population. A higher proportion of female prisoners than male prisoners came from skilled non-manual occupations.

Offences committed

The types of offences committed by convicted prisoners range from the very serious to the very minor. In 1995, the director general of the Prison Service, Derek Lewis, told the Home Affairs Select Committee, that the prison population was becoming 'more violent and more volatile'. Overall, during the last decade, there has been a decrease in the number of prisoners convicted of burglary, theft and handling, fraud and forgery and an increase in those sentenced for drug offences, robbery and sexual offences.

The table below shows the change in the numbers of prisoners convicted for all offences since 1986. It reveals an increase from eight to 13 per cent in the proportion of prisoners convicted of drug offences and a decrease from 24 per cent to 15 per cent in the proportion sentenced for burglary offences. In 1996, about one third of the sentenced prison population had been convicted of offences involving violence against the person and sex; a quarter had been convicted of property offences, including burglary and theft; 14 per cent had been convicted of robbery; and 14 per cent had been convicted of drug offences.

30 June	1986	1988	1990	1992	1994	1996
Violence against the person	7,554	8,833	7,678	7,077	7,992	9,585
Sexual offences	1,897	2,692	3,029	3,156	3,279	3,951
Burglary	8,848	7,914	5,936	5,400	5,135	6,422
Robbery	3,429	3,988	4,103	4,230	5,185	5,715
Theft, fraud & forgery	7,355	5,755	4,090	3,953	4,201	5,123
Drugs offences	2,825	3,207	3,147	3,158	3,512	5,755
Other offences	3,566	4,410	3,492	3,615	3,960	4,836

Total prison population under sentence by offence group

Sentence lengths

As the number of prisoners serving sentences for violent and drug offences has increased, so too has the average sentence length. Since 1986, the lifer population has increased from 2,194 to 3,489 and the number of prisoners serving sentences of over four years has almost doubled. However, it remains the case that over half the prison population are serving sentences of less than four years. In 1996, adult males received average sentences of 4.1 months from magistrates' courts and 26.1 months from the Crown Court. Adult females received average sentences of 3.4 months from magistrates' courts and 21.1 months from the Crown Court.

In 1996, 4,723 (11 per cent) of sentenced prisoners were serving sentences of less than six months; 2,376 (six per cent) were serving sentences of between six months and less than 12 months; 17,112 (40 per cent) were serving sentences of between 12 months and less than four years; and 18,790 (44 per cent) were serving sentences of four years and

70

over. Of this latter group, 3,489 prisoners (eight per cent) were serving life sentences.

The figures above give a 'snapshot' of the prison population on a given day. An alternative approach is to consider the 'throughput' of the prison system. This shows that most of the people sent to prison are guilty of non-violent offences. They include around 8,600 people received into prison as fine defaulters (ten per cent of all receptions under sentence in 1996).

SPECIFIC GROUPS OF PRISONER

Remand prisoners, sentenced male and sentenced female prisoners, young offenders, lifers, prisoners from ethnic minorities, foreign nationals, prisoners with mental health problems, and prisoners who must be segregated for their own safety, all form distinct but overlapping groups within the prison population. The care and custody of such a wide variety of people presents the Prison Service with a particular set of difficulties and responsibilities.

Remand prisoners
The remand population consists of two groups of prisoner: those awaiting trial and those who have been convicted but not sentenced. Unconvicted prisoners are those the courts have decided might abscond, interfere with witnesses, or commit further offences. Unsentenced prisoners are held while pre-sentence reports (PSRs) are prepared by the Probation Service which inform courts' decisions about the sentence they should receive.

For much of the 1980s, delays in bringing cases to trial fuelled a continuing rise in the number of remand prisoners. From an average of 6,438 unconvicted and unsentenced prisoners in 1980 (including an average of 645 held in police cells), the remand population reached a peak of 11,440 (including 982 in police cells) in 1988.

Since the beginning of the 1990s the rapid escalation in the number of remand prisoners has slowed, although there has been a significant rise in the number of unsentenced prisoners from 1,816 in 1990 to 3,238 in 1996.

71

Year	Untried prisoners	Unsentenced prisoners	Police cells	Total
1980	3,921	1,872	645	6,438
1981	4,804	2,101	125	7,030
1982	5,362	2,023	47	7,432
1983	6,002	1,649	310	7,961
1984	7,173	1,514	54	8,741
1985	8,132	1,565	45	9,742
1986	8,530	1,432	119	10,081
1987	9,074	1,551	537	11,162
1988	8,798	1,660	982	11,440
1989	8,576	1,820	103	10,499
1990	7,624	1,816	465	9,905
1991	7,544	1,930	683	10,157
1992	7,386	1,989	715	10,090
1993	7,960	2,700	14	10,674
1994	9,046	3,181	129	12,356
1995	8,352	2,954	68	11,374
1996	8,375	3,238	-	11,613

Average population of remand prisoners in custody 1980-1996

In 1996 there was an average of 11,600 prisoners held on remand. Of these, 72 per cent were unconvicted and 28 per cent were unsentenced prisoners.

Waiting for trial
Some untried remand prisoners spend over a year in prison before their cases come to trial. In 1996, untried male prisoners spent an average of 53 days in custody (down from 59 days in 1994), while untried female prisoners spent an average of 41 days (down from a peak of 51 days in 1988). However, these averages mask the very long periods which significant numbers of remand prisoners spend waiting for trial. On 30 June 1996, there were 1,200 prisoners (14 per cent of the total untried population) who were first received on remand more than six months previously. Of these, 250 had been first remanded more than 12 months previously.

Trial outcomes
Fewer than half the males remanded in custody, and fewer than one-third of the women, are subsequently given a custodial sentence. In 1996, around 24 per cent of males and females were acquitted or the proceedings terminated early. Of the males who were convicted, only 46 per cent received a sentence of immediate custody; of the convicted females, only 31 per cent received such a sentence.

Profile of remand prisoners
The data shows that:

- average age of remand prisoners in 1996 was 27. About one-quarter of remand prisoners are under the age of 21.
- in 1996, women represented 4.6 per cent of the total remand population, a figure which has risen consistently since 1993.
- the number of juveniles held on remand increased from 1,266 in 1990 to 1,889 in 1995.
- the proportion of male prisoners from minority ethnic groups who are on remand is greater than for whites. On 30 June 1996, 24 per cent of black male prisoners were held on remand, compared with 21 per cent of white males. However, the proportion of black women on remand is lower than for whites.

Remand prisoners experience some of the poorest regimes in the prison system; and many unconvicted prisoners experience anxieties about their immediate future. In particular, they experience uncertainty about whether they will be found guilty or not, uncertainty about the sentence they might receive and uncertainty about their personal and business affairs. They are a particularly vulnerable group. In the year ending 31 March 1995, 2,481 psychiatric assessments were prepared on defendants remanded in custody. In 1996, 56 per cent of self-inflicted deaths involved prisoners on remand.

Adult male prisoners
Over half the prison population is made up of adult male prisoners under sentence. In 1996, there was a total of 34,960 such prisoners, nearly a quarter of whom had been convicted of violence against the person, 15 per cent of drug offences, 14 per cent of burglary and 13 per cent of robbery.

30 June	1986	1988	1990	1992	1994	1996
Violence against the person	5,702	6,867	6,458	6,178	6,869	8,116
Sexual offences	1,703	2,463	2,801	2,985	3,138	3,787
Burglary	5,448	5,209	4,232	3,989	3,740	4,685
Robbery	2,429	2,946	3,152	3,377	4,262	4,346
Theft, fraud & forgery	5,325	4,260	3,169	3,167	3,258	3,973
Drug offences	2,481	2,760	2,739	2,776	3,050	4,965
Other offences	2,487	3,172	2,651	2,817	3,222	3,957

Adult men in prison under sentence by offence group

73

Over the past decade the proportion serving sentences of over four years has increased from 29 per cent to 42 per cent, while the proportion serving sentences of 12 months or less has decreased from 25 per cent to 18 per cent.

Adult women prisoners

The number of women prisoners has increased at twice the rate as the number of men in recent years. Between 1992 and 1997 the average number of women in prison increased from 1,562 to 2,675, an increase of 71 per cent. Notwithstanding, women remain a minority in prison, representing about only six per cent of the total prison population.

In keeping with the overall trend for men, there has been an increase in the number of women prisoners convicted of offences involving drugs and violence and a decrease in the number convicted of theft and fraud. In 1996 nearly a third (32 per cent) were serving sentences for drug offences, 28 per cent for theft and fraud offences and 20 per cent for violence against the person.

30 June	1986	1988	1990	1992	1994	1996
Violence against the person	150	191	170	158	238	288
Sexual offences	10	14	9	9	12	10
Burglary	55	36	40	40	30	52
Robbery	33	48	31	37	72	79
Theft, fraud & forgery	384	278	231	224	275	397
Drug offences	208	305	303	245	313	451
Other offences	89	146	188	143	108	136

Adult women in prison under sentence by offence group

Consequently, the proportion of women serving longer sentences has also increased. Between 1986 and 1996 the number of women serving sentences of longer than three years increased from 22 per cent to 40 per cent, while the proportion serving sentences of up to 18 months decreased from 54 per cent to 39 per cent.

Profile of women prisoners
It is generally accepted that the position of women prisoners differs markedly from that of men. They serve shorter sentences; a far greater proportion of women prisoners are first offenders (or are in custody for the first time) and the number convicted of crimes of violence is much lower. The numbers of foreign nationals are much greater. The proportion with drug problems is much higher. Also a far greater

74

proportion of women than male prisoners have primary child care responsibilities. Recent surveys of women prisoners have found that:

- about 30 per cent of women prisoners are aged under 25, compared to 13 per cent in the general population;
- just over two-thirds of women prisoners have never been in prison before;
- just over two-thirds of women prisoners are mothers with an average of three children; 55 per cent of women prisoners have a first child during their teens, compared to 20 per cent in the general population; 47 per cent of women prisoners have dependent children compared with 32 per cent of men; one in ten of the children born to women prisoners are in local authority or foster care;
- twenty seven per cent of women prisoners are single mothers compared to eight per cent in the general population;
- about 70 per cent of women have no previous employment experience prior to prison; and over a third are in debt;
- women from ethnic minorities are disproportionately represented; and about 13 per cent of women prisoners are foreign nationals.

Research has also found that about one fifth of women have experienced time in local authority care. Nearly half of women prisoners have been either physically or sexually abused at some point in their lives. Two thirds have used illegal drugs and 40 per cent admit to heavy use of drugs or addiction.

The behaviour of women in prison also differs markedly from that of men. Although women prisoners may exhibit disturbed and disruptive behaviour, concerted activity by groups of women prisoners is rare. Women prisoners do not riot and the escape/abscond rate is much lower for women than for men.

Of all prison suicides in England and Wales between 1972 and 1987, 1.7 per cent involved women. Although the female suicide rate is broadly on a par with that of men, levels of self injury are usually much higher. Surveys have shown that over 40 per cent of women admit to having harmed themselves intentionally and/or to having attempted suicide. This is generally thought to be because women are more likely than men to direct distress and frustration inwardly.

Young offenders
Young people are responsible for a disproportionate amount of crime committed each year. The peak age of offending for males is 18, for females it is 15. Thereafter, research suggests that offending begins to

75

tail off in the mid to late 20s, although perhaps to a lesser degree than used to be the case.

Between 1980 and 1993 the number of young offenders in prison fell by half. Since 1993, the number of young offenders in prison has increased by 30 per cent. In 1996 there was an average of 6,615 sentenced young offenders in prison. Of these, 1,320 (20 per cent) were aged 17 years or under and 252 were female. In addition, 2,900 young offenders were held on remand.

Reasons for the increase include the harsher sentencing climate which has prevailed since 1993. Although the official statistics suggest juvenile crime has fallen, there has been increased public anxiety about teenage crime. This has been the case particularly since the abduction and murder of a toddler, James Bulger, by two ten year old boys in 1993.

Only a small number of young people commit very serious crimes. Although, over the last decade there has been an increase in the proportion of young offenders serving sentences for robbery, sexual offences and drugs offences and a decrease in the proportion serving sentences for burglary, theft and fraud, the most common offence committed by young people in custody remains burglary. In 1996, 26 per cent of male young offenders were serving sentences for burglary, 20 per cent for robbery, 18 per cent for violence against the person and 11 per cent for theft and handling. The proportion of female young offenders serving sentences for drug offences in 1996 was 22 per cent.

30 June	1986	1988	1990	1992	1994	1996
Violence against the person	1,646	1,719	1,019	715	846	1,114
Sexual offences	182	214	217	161	129	152
Burglary	3,310	2,648	1,653	1,360	1,356	1,657
Robbery	935	969	900	797	828	1,245
Theft, fraud & forgery	1,570	1,182	673	543	651	717
Drug offences	119	133	90	123	136	304
Other offences	962	1,068	629	640	606	715

Young offenders in prison under sentence by offence group

In 1996, just under a half of young offenders were serving sentences of up to 18 months, just under a third were serving sentences of 18 months to three years and 21 per cent were serving sentences of longer than three years. The average length of time actually spent in custody was 4.4 months.

76

Profile of young offenders
Recent surveys have shown that:

- only one in ten young offenders in prison have no previous convictions;
- of all young offenders discharged from custody in 1993, 75 per cent were re-convicted and 46 per cent recommitted to prison within two years;
- many young offenders have been in local authority care or been in contact with the social services prior to their imprisonment;
- seventeen per cent admit to having suffered physical or sexual abuse;
- one in ten admit to having harmed themselves while in prison, frequently as a result of bullying;
- the numbers of young people committing suicide in prisons is increasing. In 1996, 22 per cent of self inflicted deaths occurred amongst prisoners aged 21 or under;
- about two thirds of young offenders have no educational qualifications; and two thirds were unemployed prior to going to prison. Those with work experience were unskilled and had received little or no training;
- about two thirds admit to having used drugs and about one-quarter had been under the influence of alcohol at the time of their arrest.

Life sentenced prisoners
Since the abolition of the death penalty as the punishment for murder in 1965, the number of prisoners serving life sentences in prison has increased steadily. Between 1986 and 1996, the number of lifers increased from 2,194 to 3,489, an increase of nearly 60 per cent.

30 June	1986	1988	1990	1992	1994	1996
Total population	2,194	2,503	2,795	3,000	3,192	3,489
Males	2,126	2,427	2,704	2,904	3,081	3,365
Females	68	76	91	96	111	124

Population of life sentenced prisoners

In 1996, male prisoners accounted for 96 per cent of life sentenced prisoners. About 81 per cent of male lifers had been convicted of murder, six per cent of manslaughter, other homicide or attempted

77

homicide, and seven per cent of rape or other sexual offences. The remainder had been convicted of robbery, arson and other offences.

About 83 per cent of the small number of female lifers had been convicted of murder. The remainder had been convicted of arson (eight per cent), homicide (six per cent), manslaughter (three per cent) and violence against the person (less than one per cent).

All prisoners serving life sentences remain in prison for an indeterminate period of time. This means they are released only when it is considered safe to do so. All lifers who are released remain 'on licence' to the probation service for the rest of their lives and may be recalled to prison if they commit further offences or breach the conditions of their licence.

During the past ten years the average length of time served by released life sentenced prisoners has increased from 10.7 years in 1985 to 13.9 years in 1996. The number of prisoners serving life sentences of 15 years or over has also increased. Between 1975 and 1996 the number of lifers serving between ten and 15 years increased from eight to 18 per cent and the number serving over 15 years increased from two to 16 per cent.

There are two types of life sentence: mandatory life sentences and discretionary life sentences.

Mandatory life sentences

Under the Murder (Abolition of the Death Penalty) Act 1965 it is now mandatory for life sentences to be passed by the courts on all offenders convicted of murder. Under the Crime (Sentences) Act 1997 it is also now mandatory for life sentences to be passed on all offenders convicted of a second serious violent or sexual offence.

The minimum period of time that prisoners serving mandatory life sentences remain in prison is known as the tariff. In the case of life sentences for murder, the tariff is decided by the home secretary after taking into account recommendations made by the trial judge and the Lord Chief Justice. The tariff is meant to reflect the circumstances of the offence and to satisfy the requirements of retribution and deterrence.

All life sentenced prisoners have their cases reviewed by the Parole Board three years before the end of their tariff. However, in the case of those convicted of murder, it is for the home secretary to decide when, or indeed if, prisoners serving mandatory life sentences will ever be released. In some cases, the tariff has been set at natural life. This has meant that a small group of lifers who, although they have been assessed by the Parole Board as presenting little or no risk to public safety, have nevertheless been retained in custody by successive home secretaries.

Discretionary life sentences
Discretionary life sentences may be passed by the courts on offenders convicted of a number of other serious offences including manslaughter, armed robbery, buggery, arson or rape. In contrast to mandatory life sentences, the tariff for discretionary life sentence prisoners is set by the trial judge and is subject to appeal. Once the tariff has been served the Parole Board decides whether to release or retain prisoners according to whether they continue to represent a threat to public safety. The home secretary is not involved in the decision.

Profile of life sentence prisoners
Lifers tend to be older than the general prison population. The majority are aged between 30 and 39. In 1996, 160 lifers were over 60 and the oldest was 85. Between 1989 and 1994, 59 lifers died in prison. In 1996 there were 75 lifers under the age of 21.

As a minority group, lifers often feel isolated and alienated from mainstream prison life. They may experience extreme guilt about the offence they have committed and this, together with the prospect of a long and uncertain period of imprisonment, can cause feelings of isolation, hopelessness and despair. In addition, many life sentenced prisoners quickly lose contact with the outside world, and may require intensive help in order to prepare for their release.

Prisoners of ethnic minority origin
Black people are eight times more likely to be in prison than whites. Home Office figures show that the incarceration rate for black people is 1,162 per 100,000, compared to 146 per 100,000 for whites.

Given the large numbers of prisoners of ethnic minority origin, the Prison Service has developed race relations policies which seek to ensure non-discriminatory treatment and to provide for the specific dietary requirements and religious practices of minority ethnic groups. Race Relations Management Teams (RRMTs) have been established in prisons to oversee the development of local race relations strategies and to promote racial equality and monitor performance. RRMTs usually include representatives from each prison department, a prison officer, the chaplain, a member of the Board of Visitors and representatives from local community organizations.

Most importantly, the RRMT includes a specially appointed Race Relations Liaison Officer, whose role it is to provide information to staff and prisoners on race relations policies and to monitor race relations in prisons. The role is a large one and includes the recording of racially motivated attacks, ensuring that all staff carry out race relations policies and promoting racial harmony amongst staff and prisoners.

On paper, the anti-racist policies of the Prison Service are a model for all institutions. For example, there is widespread monitoring of regimes, discipline, and cell allocation. But good practice has not been introduced uniformly and despite efforts to ensure that prisons adhere to the principles and practices of good race relations, many black prisoners say that they regularly experience racism.

Foreign nationals

In part due to the increasing ease of international travel, the number of foreign nationals held in prisons has grown dramatically in recent years. The number of foreign nationals in prison reached 4,221 at the end of April 1996. Of these, 3,917 (93 per cent) were men and 304 (seven per cent) were women; 15 per cent were Irish, 12 per cent were Jamaican, seven per cent were Pakistani and five per cent were Nigerian. However, a survey by the Prison Reform Trust found prisoners from every country from Afghanistan to Zimbabwe.

Foreign nationals account for about eight per cent of the total prison population (seven per cent of male and 14 per cent of female prisoners). In 1996, over half the women foreign nationals had been convicted of drug offences, an indication of the continuing use of women as so-called 'drug mules'.

A significant number of foreign nationals are asylum-seekers or have been detained under the Immigration Act 1971. Immigration Act detainees may not have committed an offence, but are alleged to have broken immigration rules. At the end of May 1996, there were 751 people detained in prisons or detention centres who had sought asylum. Of these, 697 (93 per cent) were men and 54 (seven per cent) were women. Although not held under a criminal charge, 475 were held in prisons; the remainder were held in privatised detention centres.

Many Immigration Act detainees have fled dangerous situations in their home countries and have few possessions or friends. Frequently they are not told how long they will remain in prison. Many become increasingly mistrustful and fearful of authority.

Many foreign nationals are unable to speak English. While the criminal justice system requires interpreters and translators to be available during police and court proceedings, there are no such requirements for the Prison Service. However, much information—including a Prison Reform Trust/Prison Service Prisoners' Information Book, which should be given to all prisoners on reception—is translated into many different languages.

80

Mentally disturbed prisoners

A significant number of prisoners are mentally disturbed. That is, they have been assessed as suffering from a range of mental illnesses including neurotic, behavioural and personality disorders, or they have learning difficulties. Home Office research suggests that more than one in three adult male prisoners suffers from some kind of psychiatric problem.

Although the government says that mentally ill people should be dealt with by the health and social services rather than in prison, in practice offenders are often held in prison in order to be assessed by a psychiatrist and only then transferred to psychiatric hospital as appropriate. People with mental health problems may also be held in prisons for the following reasons:

- some mentally ill offenders will not be identified as such until they are in prison
- often, when sentencing, it is the offence that is important to the court. People with more minor mental health problems are seen firstly as offenders and the circumstances surrounding the offence are considered to be less important
- some prisoners develop mental health problems while they are in prison
- not all mental illness falls within the definition of a 'treatable mental disorder'. In particular, many psychiatrists regard those with a psychopathic disorder as being more-or-less untreatable
- because there is a shortage of medium and high-security hospital beds, there are practical limits on how many offenders can be diverted from prison. Often the facilities are not available to make diversion a viable option.

Prisoners with mental health problems, such as depression and schizophrenia, are particularly vulnerable to suicide. A review of 69 self-inflicted deaths between January 1992 and October 1993 found that 34 (49 per cent) had a previous psychiatric history. Of these, ten prisoners (14.5 per cent) had previously been sectioned under the Mental Health Act.

Remand prisoners are particularly at risk. In 1993, the Mental Health Foundation found there were about 3,000 male and 156 female remand prisoners who had been assessed as suffering from psychiatric problems. A study of remand prisoners carried out between August 1993 and October 1994 by the Health Advisory Committee for the Prison Service found 66 per cent of adult males, 53 per cent of male youths and 77 per cent of women attracted a psychiatric diagnosis. And in the year ending 31 March 1995, 2,481 psychiatric assessments were prepared on defendants remanded in custody.

Prisoners suffering from psychiatric problems continue to form a sizeable minority of remand prisoners in spite of the fact that the Prison Service has recognised that prison conditions are not conducive to the well-being of those who are mentally ill. Research carried out for the Home Office in 1991 concluded that

> as a method of obtaining psychiatric help for mentally disordered offenders, the custodial remand has nothing to commend it; it is inhumane, expensive and ineffective. It exposes mentally disordered people to conditions and regimes which are cruelly harsh and inappropriate. It brings into prison thousands of defendants who do not need to be there and for whom penal disposals are never contemplated.

The failings of the current assessment procedures, and the length of time mentally disturbed prisoners can remain in prison before transfer continue to attract considerable criticism. A major area of criticism, which applies to all prisoners but is particularly relevant to those with mental health problems, is that the Health Care Service for Prisoners does not provide in-patient care to the standards of the National Health Service, nor indeed is it obliged to do so by law. This has led both penal reform and mental health charities to call for the integration of prison medical services with the mainstream NHS. The mental health charity, MIND, has argued that this would

> help to eliminate confusion between the Prison Service and the Health Service; help to safeguard against the indeterminate sentence; help to relieve NHS clinicians of the added burden of the moral dilemma posed by societal expectations of incarceration for mentally disordered offenders; and importantly, help to ensure that the needs of this category of offender are appropriately met.

Concern has also been expressed by HM Chief Inspector of Prisons who in 1996 reported that

> Nursing staff require more expertise in the handling of the mentally-ill, depressed and suicidal patient . . . the whole question of training and research needs to be addressed. The many mentally disordered offenders who fall outside the 1983 Mental Health Act, and are thus cared for within establishments, are not adequately provided for . . . while it is true that resources have grown, so too has the size of the problem presented by prisoners . . . In short, the pace of change within the Prison Service is dictated by the scale of the presented medical problems and it is rapidly falling behind that in the NHS.

Segregated prisoners

Prisoners may be segregated from the mainstream prison population either because they threaten to jeopardise the good order and discipline of the prison or for their own protection.

Such prisoners are commonly known as rule 43 prisoners after the Prison Rule which authorises their segregation. Rule 43 states:

> Where it appears desirable, for the maintenance of good order or discipline or in his own interests, that a prisoner should not associate with other prisoners, either generally or for particular purposes, the governor may arrange for the prisoner's removal from association accordingly.
>
> A prisoner shall not be removed under this rule for a period of more than three days without the authority of a member of the board of visitors or of the secretary of state. An authority given under this paragraph shall be for a period not exceeding one month, but may be reviewed from month to month except that, in the case of a person aged less than 21 years who is detained in prison, such an authority shall be for a period not exceeding 14 days, but may be reviewed from time to time for a like period.
>
> The governor may arrange at his discretion for such a prisoner as aforesaid to resume association with other prisoners, and shall do so if in any case the medical officer so advises on medical grounds.

In addition, rule 45 authorises the confinement of violent prisoners in special cells and rule 46 authorises governors to put prisoners under restraint 'where this is necessary to prevent the prisoner from injuring himself or others, damaging property or creating a disturbance'.

Prisoners who are segregated for their own protection are sometimes known as vulnerable prisoners. (Indeed, these days, many are held together in so-called Vulnerable Prisoner Units, rather than segregated under Prison Rule 43). The majority of such prisoners have committed offences that other prisoners strongly disapprove of, such as offences against children. Prison culture frequently involves an internal code of conduct which ranks offences according to the esteem in which certain offenders are held. Armed robbers tend to be ranked at the top of the hierarchy, while sex offenders are at the bottom. The culture of violence and intimidation which also pervades much prison life means that sex offenders are likely to be the subject of vicious verbal and physical attacks. Other vulnerable prisoners may include ex-police officers, those suspected of being informers and prisoners who are unable to pay back their debts.

Rule 43 prisoners usually live in separate units, wings or landings to other prisoners. For many, this means they are unable to take part in mainstream activities such as work and education and must spend longer periods confined to their cells.

CHAPTER 5

Prison Conditions

This chapter describes the conditions in which prisoners are held. It presents a picture of the day to day routines—the locking and unlocking, the food, the clothes—and it details the various rules and regulations to which all prisoners must adhere. Although it is the aim of the chapter to provide an account of what life is like in prison, it can only scratch the surface. Conditions vary from prison to prison and also within prisons over time. In order to gain a fuller understanding of how prisoners respond to life in prison, to understand the feelings that imprisonment may evoke, the smells, the sounds, the atmosphere of prison, it is necessary to read the accounts of ex-prisoners. For example, Oscar Wilde's poem, *The Ballad of Reading Gaol* (1898), *Borstal Boy* by Brendan Behan (1958), *A Sense of Freedom* by Jimmy Boyle (1977), *A Product of the System* by Mark Leech (1992) and *I'm Still Standing* by Bob Turney contain personal accounts of experiences of imprisonment over the past 100 years.

For many first time prisoners the unique physical and cultural environment of prison can be a shocking experience. In closed prisons the buildings are often enormous and uninviting. The rules and regulations are complex and bewildering. The routines that are necessary to move prisoners around—the systematic unlocking and locking of all doors, the escorting of groups of prisoners along corridors and landings, the regular meal times—are strict and impersonal. The lack of freedom, the powerlessness, the isolation, the separation from friends and family and the outside world are features of prison life to which all first time prisoners must quickly become accustomed.

PHYSICAL CONDITIONS

Cells

A small number of prisons have dormitory style accommodation, but most prisoners are kept in cells. Closed prisons are divided into wings and each wing has a number of levels or landings which contain the cells. The number of cells on each landing varies from prison to prison and from wing to wing.

The cell is where prisoners live. It is a bedroom, living area, dining room and toilet all rolled into one. Most single cells contain a bed, table, chair, lavatory, wash-basin, a tiny barred window and some shelf space. The doors to most cells are made of metal and can only be opened from the outside. Each door has a tiny aperture for surveillance. When prisons become overcrowded, prisoners may be kept two to a cell (or three to a two-person cell). Many of those who share cells sleep on bunk beds.

Cell sizes vary, but most are cramped. The recommended minimum size is 59.2 square feet, although some cells are smaller. For example, Eastwood Park, a women's prison near Bristol, contains some cells which are 36 feet square. There are also standards for ventilation, lighting and heating in cells, although prisoners cannot enforce these standards through the courts.

Prisoners are required to keep their cells clean and tidy. Cells which are occupied by more than one prisoner can quickly become dirty. All floors must be scrubbed once a week and all interior walls cleaned once every six months.

In-cell sanitation

Although many Victorian prisons were originally built with integral sanitation, a prevailing image of prison is 'slopping out'—the use of a plastic bucket as a toilet. Prisoners had to use a chamber pot, which was emptied once a day, usually in the mornings. Until it was finally ended in April 1996, 'slopping out' had come to symbolise the squalid and decrepit conditions in prisons.

Improvements to sanitation in closed prisons have been achieved for the most part through the installation of in-cell sanitation. Although generally considered to be a major improvement to the quality of life for both prisoners and staff, the decision to install in-cell sanitation has nevertheless provoked criticism. In particular, integral sanitation has reduced available cell space and, because adequate screening has not been installed, prisoners sharing cells have been required—in effect—to live in communal toilets.

Personal hygiene

Clothes

According to the Prison Rules prisoners should be provided with clothing that is adequate for warmth and good health. Most convicted male prisoners are required to wear prison issue clothing which consists of blue trousers and blue-and-white thin striped shirts. A small number of convicted prisoners are allowed to wear their own clothes as a privilege under the Incentives and Earned Privileges Scheme (see Chapter 6).

Remand prisoners and women prisoners are also allowed to wear their own clothes, although remand prisoners must first ensure they will be supplied with clean clothes on a regular basis by their visitors.

Washing facilities are available in some training prisons to enable convicted prisoners to wash their own clothes.

Showers
Few prisoners have the opportunity to take a daily shower as they might at home. Access to baths and showers is very limited. However, all prisoners are required to shower or take a bath at least once a week.

Hair care
All prisoners are supposed to have their hair cut regularly for reasons of neatness, health and safety. In practice, this rule is rarely enforced. Remand prisoners and women prisoners are not required to have their hair cut unless the medical officer requests it for medical reasons. All male prisoners are required to shave daily, unless they already have a beard, and they should be supplied with clean razors every day.

Food
The Prison Service Operating Standards state that prisoners should be provided with a varied and healthy diet which reflects modern eating habits, and official advice about healthy eating. Meals should be varied, nutritious and cooked to approved standards. Vegetarians, vegans and people with religious dietary needs are catered for, as are those who require a special medical diet, such as diabetics.

Prison food has improved considerably since the early 1990s. At the time of the 1990-91 Woolf Inquiry prison food was reported as being 'inedible' and 'monotonous'. But an inquiry into prison food conducted in 1997 by the National Audit Office, *Prison Catering, Report by the Comptroller and Auditor General*, found that—considering prisons spend on average only £1.37 a day to feed each prisoner three meals—the food was 'acceptable'.

Since 1990, when the Food Safety Act removed Crown immunity from prisons in respect of food, prison kitchens have been subject to the same food regulations as all other catering establishments. Prison caterers are able to supplement the daily food allowance with fresh produce, such as vegetables, milk, pork and eggs from the Prison Service's farms and gardens.

As in other institutions like schools and hospitals, food is an important part of prison life. In overcrowded prisons where levels of frustration can run high, food that is plentiful and varied can have a stabilising influence on prisoners. The National Audit Office found that

> mealtimes in prisons are a potential flash point. While poor quality food usually leads to customer dissatisfaction in any environment, in a prison it

can result in antisocial behaviour and, in the worst case, to disturbance and violence.

The following is a typical menu from Long Lartin prison, a high security dispersal prison in Worcestershire. It was described by the National Audit Office as 'satisfactory':

Breakfast	boiled egg, toast, marmalade, or cereals, toast, marmalade, or porridge, toast, marmalade.
Lunch	macaroni cheese, or quiche, or sausage roll (with potato/rice and bread)
Tea	vegetable stir fry, or roast pork and gravy, or braised liver and onions, or French bread pizza.

The National Audit Office was less complimentary about the times of the day that food is served in prisons, and about the fact that meals are often served more than two hours after being prepared. In order to accommodate staff working patterns, breakfast in most prisons is served at 8 a.m., lunch at 11:30 a.m. and the evening meal often as early as between 4 and 4:30 p.m. This contravenes the Prison Service standard of a maximum of 14 hours between evening meals and breakfast. As food is mostly served to prisoners in their cells and has to be wheeled on trolleys along corridors from the kitchens, by the time it reaches the cells it is sometimes either lukewarm or cold.

PRISONERS' RIGHTS

By its very nature, imprisonment takes away from prisoners the right to liberty. But in English law, a prisoner 'retains all civil rights which are not taken away expressly or by necessary implication' (Lord Wilberforce in *Raymond v. Honey* (1982)). However, although this implies that prisoners have rights, it does not delineate what rights these are, and the extent to which they can be removed.

The Prison Act 1952 places few obligations on the prison authorities and the Prison Rules were not designed to be enforced in the courts. However, prisoners have successfully challenged prison regulations both in the domestic courts and in Europe. Article 5 of the Universal

87

Declaration of Human Rights forbids torture and 'cruel, inhuman or degrading treatment or punishment'. Action through the European Commission on Human Rights has resulted in new rights for prisoners regarding correspondence, access to lawyers, and the procedures for determining the release of life sentenced prisoners. It is probable that incorporation of the European Convention on Human Rights into domestic law, likely to take place over the next few years, will enhance the ability of prisoners to obtain legal redress for their grievances.

Many of the rights that prisoners retain are described in the Prison Rules. The remainder of this chapter contains a description of various rules, regulations and requirements including those which allow prisoners to:

- maintain contact with the outside world
- practise their religion
- receive payment for prison work
- vote (if they are unconvicted); and
- receive a fair hearing if charged with an offence against prison discipline.

Maintaining contact with the outside world
A key goal of the Prison Service is to help prisoners prepare for their return to the community; and a central element in achieving this is the availability of opportunities for prisoners to maintain contact with their families. The Prison Service *Annual Report* for 1992/93 states that contact with family and friends '. . . helps [prisoners] to cope with the harsh realities of life in prison and reduces their feelings of isolation and deprivation. This contact needs to start from the initial remand and be kept up until release'.

Prisoners maintain contact with the outside world in four main ways: through writing and receiving letters, through making telephone calls, receiving visitors, and through temporary release (what used to be known as home leave).

Letters
Limits are imposed on the amount of correspondence that convicted prisoners may send or receive. There are no such limits for remand prisoners.

Remand prisoners are allowed to send two letters a week paid for by the Prison Service and others at their own expense. If remand prisoners do not have access to private cash, the Prison Service will also pay for any letters connected with the preparation of their cases.

Convicted prisoners are able to send one letter a week paid for by the Prison Service and others at their own expense. Convicted prisoners are also entitled to send free letters if they are to be transferred, if they have family or business problems, if they are involved in legal action, or if they are applying for a job or arranging accommodation.

All incoming mail is searched routinely and is sometimes read by prison staff. Letters may be read at the discretion of the governor to ensure they do not contain threats, blackmail, racially abusive or obscene language, or material which would threaten prison security. Letters sent to or received from solicitors or the Prisons Ombudsman (see *Chapter 7*) carry special privileges and are not read by prison staff.

Prisoners may write letters to newspapers and contribute to radio and TV programmes, as long as they receive no payment. However, they must not express any personal opinions about their offences, unless the reason for doing so is to make 'serious comment' about the nature of crime or the workings of the criminal justice system.

Telephone calls
Prisoners may make telephone calls from card-operated pay phones during hours specified by the governor. All phone cards must be purchased from the prison shop, i.e. they must not be sent in by family or friends (indeed, ordinary phone cards do not work in prison phones). In each prison, limits on the number of phone cards which can be bought are set by the Incentives and Earned Privileges Scheme (see *Chapter 6*). Prisoners are not allowed to receive incoming calls.

Communication by telephone is subject to the same restrictions as correspondence. Category A prisoners must submit a list of people they wish to call for approval and their calls are tightly monitored. Prisoners are not allowed to telephone any of the victims of their offences unless the victim is a close relative, the victim has first approached the prisoner, or the governor is satisfied the call would not cause distress. In addition, prisoners are not permitted to make calls to radio phone-in programmes.

Visits
In its evidence to the Woolf Inquiry, the Prison Service described the importance of visits to prisoners and their families as follows:

> The disruption of the inmate's position within the family unit represents one of the most distressing aspects of imprisonment . . . Enabling inmates, so far as possible, to stay in close and meaningful contact with the family is therefore an essential part of humane treatment . . . There is every reason to believe that the nature of a prisoner's relationships with his or her family will be an important factor in determining whether he or she will succeed in leading a useful and law-abiding life on return to the community.

The importance of helping prisoners to maintain links with the community has been recognised by the Prison Service to the extent that prisoners are allowed to receive visitors as frequently as circumstances in each prison permit. Convicted prisoners are entitled to a minimum of two visits of one hour duration every month. In addition, there are opportunities for prisoners to earn extra visits through the Incentives and Earned Privileges Scheme by demonstrating good behaviour. Governors may also allow special visits from legal advisers, probation officers etc. which do not normally count against a prisoner's entitlement.

Remand prisoners are entitled to a minimum of one-and-a-half hours of visits every week. Most local prisons allow more than this if staffing levels permit. Governors decide the times and the duration of the visits, although all remand prisoners should have visits on at least three days of the week and there should be a visit on a Saturday or Sunday at least once a fortnight.

All visitors to convicted prisoners must be in possession of a visiting order, which is sent to them by the prisoners they wish to visit and is valid for a specified period of time. Visiting orders are used for identification purposes and to monitor the number of visits each prisoner receives. Many prisons also insist that visits are pre-booked. This is usually done by the visitor who must telephone the prison to arrange a suitable time.

Most visits take place in a large visits room within the prison. There is normally a play area for children and a refreshments counter. Visits should take place within sight, but not within hearing, of prison officers. Up to three adults and the prisoner's children are normally allowed at each visit. Prisoners are normally allowed to embrace their visitors.

All visitors to prison may be asked to undergo a search. This usually includes a 'rub-down' which should be carried out by an officer of the same sex. Until recently all visitors had to be searched by officers of the same sex, but now men may be searched by women. Searches are intended to prevent drugs and firearms from entering the prison and may be carried out without the visitor's consent. If visitors refuse to be searched, or if prisoners have been found in possession of drugs, the prison may either refuse the visit, or insist that it is conducted under 'no-contact' or 'closed' conditions. Prisoners subject to 'no-contact visits' are permitted no physical contact with their visitors, while closed visits stipulate that prisoners and their visitors are physically separated by a screen.

The cost of travelling to many prisons can be prohibitive. Although the Woolf Report recommended that prisoners should be held in prisons near to their homes, an effect of recent overcrowding has been that many prisoners are now held in faraway prisons where space is available. Frequently, this means that families and friends face strenuous journeys at considerable cost in order to visit them. The Assisted Prisons Visits Unit within the Prison Service provides some financial assistance to close relatives of prisoners who are receiving income support, family credit or a disability working allowance. Alternatively, convicted prisoners may accumulate between three and 26 visits and apply to be temporarily moved to a prison nearer to their homes for a period of up to 28 days in order to have the visits they have accumulated. Prisoners can apply for 'accumulated visits' once every six months.

Religion
Prisoners have the right to practise a religion, as long as it is one recognised by the Prison Service. All religious practices, including diet and dress, are observed. A number of faiths are not recognised, including Rastafarianism.

The observance of the Christian religion is enshrined in the Prison Act 1952, which makes provision for the appointment of chaplains. Minority Christian faiths such as Christian Science, Mormonism, Jehovah's Witnesses and Seventh-Day Adventists are also recognised.

It was a feature of nineteenth century prisons that they were designed with the chapel at their heart. Today, many chapels are used as multi-faith centres, offering opportunities for the ministers of many different religions to provide spiritual and pastoral care to prisoners. Reflecting Britain's multi-cultural and multi-faith society, there are increasing numbers of Moslems, Hindus, Sikhs, Jews and Buddhists in prison.

In every prison a Chaplaincy Team, which normally consists of chaplains from the Church of England, the Roman Catholics and the Methodists, provide pastoral care to prisoners and attempt to ensure that prisons are functioning in a just and humane manner. An important duty of chaplains is to visit prisoners who are ill or who are confined to their cell every day.

One prison chaplain has described the role that he and his colleagues play in the following terms:

A chaplain is a servant of the Church first but also a civil servant. This lays upon the chaplain an obligation not only to work within the system but also to work to change the system, to question and challenge it, if and when it becomes necessary. Yet there is also the need to be seen to be independent of the system. Such neutrality is destroyed if one is locked too closely into the prison management system. Nevertheless, the physical requirements to carry keys identifies chaplains with the system – a compromise which has to be accepted in spite of misunderstanding it might create. Keys also open doors.

Pay

All convicted prisoners are required to work for which they are paid accordingly. Earnings, which are usually at pocket money level, are used to buy items such as cigarettes and sweets from the prison shop. Convicted prisoners who are in education or training, or who are prevented from working due to illness, or for whom no work is available, instead receive a small allowance. Convicted prisoners who refuse to work are subject to disciplinary proceedings and receive no payment for the period of their unemployment. Remand prisoners are not required to work. However, they receive no allowance if work is available and they opt to remain unemployed.

In 1991, the Woolf Report found that pay levels for prisoners were too low and that pay was a substantial cause of disquiet and dissatisfaction within prisons. Prior to 1991, the basic rate of pay was £1.75 and the maximum wage was £5.87 per week. The Woolf Report concluded:

> There are strong arguments for providing additional pay for prisoners . . . A reasonable level of pay enables a prison to provide a sensible level of incentives, reflecting more accurately a range of effort and achievement. Pay is often seen in life outside prison as some measure of a person's worth. It is understandable that a similar yardstick should be applied by prisoners to prison wages . . . A more realistic level of pay would also allow prisoners to exercise some of the responsibilities that will be expected of them on release.

Following Woolf's recommendations there was an 8.5 per cent increase in all pay rates and in unemployment pay. Today, prisoners are paid according to a variety of different pay schemes, depending on the type of job they perform. On average, prisoners receive a weekly wage of between £7 and £8. Prisoners who work in the kitchens tend to receive higher than average rates of pay. A small number of prisoners who work for private sector employers receive pay at, or close to, commercial rates.

There are strong arguments for offering prisoners the opportunity to earn more realistic levels of pay. As well as the Woolf Report, HM Chief Inspector of Prisons, penal reform groups and prisoners themselves have all argued that low rates of pay do not provide sufficient incentive for prisoners to work hard and that they cause, rather than reflect, the low productivity and low profitability of prison industries. Increasing rates of pay would enable prisoners to support their families financially, to contribute to the board-and-lodging costs of keeping them in prison, to make reparation to their victims and to save money for their release.

Private cash
Prisoners are entitled to receive private cash from their own savings or from their families. The amount is determined by the Incentives and Earned Privileges Scheme. Convicted prisoners are entitled to receive £2.50, £10 or £15 per week, depending on whether they are on the basic, standard or enhanced privilege levels of the scheme. Remand prisoners are entitled to receive £15 on the basic level or £30 on the enhanced level.

Voting rights
The right to vote is expressly taken away from convicted prisoners under section 3(1) Representation of the People Act 1983. The loss of enfranchisement applies to prisoners who have been convicted by the courts of criminal offences. It does not apply to remand prisoners, or to so-called civil prisoners—maintenance defaulters and the like.

The right of prisoners to vote differs from country to country. In 1994, of 34 countries which responded to a survey carried out by Penal Reform International on the issue, 18 allowed prisoners to vote, whereas in 16 the right to take part in democratic elections had been removed.

Countries in which convicted prisoners retain the vote	Countries in which convicted prisoners lose the vote
Australia	Brazil
Canada	Chile
Croatia	Czech Republic
Cyprus	Egypt
Denmark	Hungary
France	Italy
Germany	Japan
India	Jordan
The Netherlands	Kenya
New Zealand	Lesotho
Norway	Pakistan
Peru	Russia
Poland	Senegal
Romania	Uganda
South Africa	United Kingdom
Sweden	USA
Trinidad and Tobago	
Zimbabwe	

93

In Britain, at the 1995 Trades Union Congress, the National Association of Probation Officers (NAPO) proposed the following motion regarding a prisoner's right to vote:

> Congress notes that convicted prisoners are amongst a very small number of other groups, including peers of the realm, who are excluded under the Representation of the People Act from the right to vote.
>
> Congress believes that banning convicted prisoners from the right to vote:
> — is an unnecessary denial of a basic human right;
> — excludes prisoners further from taking their share of responsibility within society; and
> — reduces the level of concern amongst many MPs about conditions for prisoners.
>
> Congress therefore calls on the General Council to campaign for a change in legislation in order to provide convicted prisoners with the right to vote.

The TUC voted in favour of the motion by 3,932,000 to 2,265,000, a majority of 1,667,000. However, the resolution was dismissed by Jack Straw on behalf of the Labour Party.

Prison discipline

Prison Rule 47 lists 22 offences against discipline. Prisoners are guilty of an offence against prison discipline if they:

1. Commit any assault;
2. Detain any person against his/her will;
3. Deny access to any part of the prison to an officer or any person (other than a prisoner) who is at the prison in order to work there;
4. Fight with any person;
5. Intentionally endanger the health or personal safety of others or, by their conduct, are reckless whether such health or personal safety is endangered;
6. Intentionally obstruct an officer in the execution of his/her duty — or any person (other than a prisoner) who is at the prison in order to work there — in performance of his/her work;
7. Escape or abscond from prison or from legal custody;
8. Fail to comply with any condition upon which they are temporarily released under rule 6 of the Prison Rules;
8a Administer a controlled drug to themselves or fail to prevent the administration of a controlled drug to themselves by another person, unless it was administered to them lawfully in the course of lawful (prescribed) administration of the drug, where they had no reason to suspect that an unlawful drug was being administered, or where it was administered under duress and it was not reasonable to resist;

9. Have in their possession-
(a) any unauthorised article; or
(b) a greater quantity of any article than they are authorised to have;
10. Sell or deliver to any person any unauthorised article;
11. Sell or, without permission, deliver to any person any article which they are allowed to have only for their own use;
12. Take improperly any article belonging to another person or to a prison;
13. Intentionally or recklessly set fire to any part of a prison or any other property, whether or not their own;
14. Destroy or damage any part of a prison or any other property other than their own;
15. Absent themselves from any place where they are required to be — or are present at any place where they are not authorised to be;
16. Are disrespectful to any officer or any person (other than a prisoner) who is at the prison in order to work there or any person visiting a prison;
17. Use threatening, abusive or insulting words or behaviour;
18. Intentionally fail to work properly or, being required to work, refuse to do so;
19. Disobey any lawful order;
20. Disobey or refuse to comply with any rule or regulation applying to them;
21. In any way offend against good order and discipline;
22. (a) attempt to commit
(b) incite another prisoner to commit, or
(c) assist another prisoner to commit or attempt to commit, any of the foregoing offences.

The number of offences against prison discipline has increased steadily in recent years, rising from about 70,000 per year during the 1980s to 115,000 in 1996.

Offences against discipline in prison include offences which outside of prison would normally not be charged under criminal law. In addition, rules 47(19), (20), (21) are 'catch-all' offences in that they penalise conduct which is not specified. Research carried out in 1995 for the Prison Reform Trust found that such rules frequently act against the interests of justice and leave both prisoners and staff unsure of what constitutes a disciplinary offence. For example, one prisoner was charged with throwing snowballs, another for playing a piano and another for 'attempting' to provoke a prison dog (it seems the animal was not provoked successfully).

Adjudications and punishments
Prisoners who are charged with an offence have the right to present their case during an adjudication. After they have been charged prisoners have at least two hours to prepare their case before the

95

adjudication takes place. They are entitled to prepare a written statement and may call witnesses to speak on their behalf. They may also be accompanied at the hearing by a solicitor (although this theoretical right is all but unknown in practice) or a 'McKenzie friend' to help them prepare their case.

The adjudicator at the hearing is a prison governor. After hearing from the prison officer who placed the prisoner 'on report', the prisoner and any witnesses to the charge, the governor decides on a verdict. If prisoners feel that they have not received a fair hearing they have the right to appeal. Their complaints are either reviewed by the area manager, Prison Service headquarters or, ultimately, by the Prisons Ombudsman.

If prisoners are found guilty, governors may impose a range of punishments. For adult prisoners these are:

- caution
- forfeiture of privileges for a period not exceeding 42 days
- exclusion from associated work for a period not exceeding 21 days
- stoppage of or deduction from earnings for a period not exceeding 84 days of an amount not exceeding 42 days' earnings
- cellular confinement for a period not exceeding 14 days
- in the case of a short-term or long-term prisoner, an award of additional days not exceeding 42 days
- in the case of a prisoner otherwise entitled to them, forfeiture for any period of the right to have books, newspapers, writing materials and other means of occupation
- in the case of a prisoner guilty of escaping or attempting to escape and who is entitled to it, forfeiture of the right to wear his own clothing.

There are a range of less severe punishments for young offenders. For example, prisoners under the age of 21 may have only 21 additional days added to their sentence and have their earnings stopped for only 21 days.

In 1996, some 115,500 offences against prison discipline were punished. The most common offences were disobedience/disrespect and unauthorised transactions/use (including possession and unauthorised use of controlled drugs). Disobedience/disrespect accounted for 40 per cent, unauthorised transactions/use for 33 per cent, and offences involving violence for about 11 per cent of all offences.

The most common form of punishment is to add days to the prisoner's sentence, followed by forfeiture of privileges and stoppage or reduction of earnings. In 1996, there were around 77,321 awards of additional days imposed on prisoners as a punishment for offences against prison discipline.

Restraints

Restraints, such as handcuffs, ankle straps, canvas jackets and body belts may be used to control prisoners who are behaving violently or considered likely to injure themselves or others. Prisoners may only be restrained for medical reasons on the order of a medical officer, or otherwise on the order of the governor.

Handcuffs and ankle straps may be used to secure disruptive prisoners during escort. Canvas jackets may only be used on the written authorisation of a medical officer. The body belt is a thick leather belt which is fastened around the prisoner's waist and which has handcuffs (iron for men, leather for women) attached to a ring on either side. Prisoners restrained by a body belt are unable to fully extend their arms. The prisoner's feet may also be tethered with leather straps.

Special and unfurnished (stripped) cells may also be used for the temporary confinement of prisoners who are deemed in need of restraint and isolation. A stripped cell is a normal cell which contains no furniture other than a mattress. A padded cell contains no furniture whatsoever, is sound proofed and has walls which are protected by thick rubber padding. Special cells are equipped with cardboard furniture that has been specially designed so as to cause no injury.

The use of restraints increased nearly two and a half times between 1988 and 1994, since when their use has levelled off. In 1996, there were 2,927 prisoners who were restrained. Of these, 338 were restrained on medical grounds and 2,553 were restrained for other reasons.

According to the Prison Rules, restraints should only be used outside of prison to prevent escape and to ensure the safe custody of prisoners. There are separate rules for pregnant female prisoners and for other prisoners who are sent to hospital. During 1996/7 the use of so-called closeting chains on sick and pregnant prisoners who had been released to hospital became the focus of intense media attention. Women were chained shortly after giving birth or during examinations for cancer. Following the case of Geoffrey Thomas, a terminally ill prisoner who remained shackled to a hospice bed until only a few hours before his death, the Prison Service conducted an internal inquiry. This in turn led to the recognition that restraints were being used inappropriately. Richard Tilt, director general of the Prison Service, commented that

security is important, but it should never blind us to the overriding need for compassion and humanity.

97

In 1997, the Prison Service revised its policy on the use of restraints. Prison governors are now expected to establish and maintain good working relationships with hospitals and to carry out risk assessments on all prisoners released to hospital based on the following factors:

- The prisoner's medical condition. The prison medical officer must be asked to advise on any medical objections to the use of restraints and the prisoner's ability to escape unaided.
- The prisoner's category.
- The nature of offences, the risk to the public and hospital staff, including the risk of hostage taking.
- The prisoner's motivation to escape, likelihood of outside assistance, and conduct while in custody.
- The physical security of the hospital, including the consulting room and where possible, other areas where tests or treatment are taking place.

The continuous assessment scheme
If prisoners are considered particularly disruptive or a threat to good order they may be placed on the Continuous Assessment Scheme (CAS) which involves moving prisoners from one segregation block to another every 28 days. At the end of July 1997, there were 40 prisoners on the CAS—or 'magic roundabout' as it is commonly referred to in prison—some of whom had been moved constantly from prison to prison for more than two years, often at little or no notice to themselves or their families.

A series of special units has also been set up to take prisoners regarded as disruptive. Prisoners may be placed in special units if they have:

- been violent to staff and/or prisoners;
- regularly incurred disciplinary reports;
- caused serious damage to property;
- shown dangerous behaviour, such as roof-top protests or hostage-taking;
- a history of mental abnormality;
- failed to respond to earlier measures to improve control.

However, critics of these arrangements say that prisoners may become more disruptive if they are treated punitively. Segregation may breed bitterness and a sense of grievance against the prison authorities.

Medical conditions

The Health Care Service for Prisoners

Prisoners experience extremely high rates of sickness. Nearly, ten per cent of the prison population ask to see a doctor every day. Undoubtedly, part of the reason for this is that prisoners want to break the monotony of prison life. They also do not have the same opportunity as the rest of society to purchase proprietory medicines. But the stresses and strains of imprisonment, the lack of exercise and fresh air, also result in prisoners being more prone to illness than the general population.

The Health Care Service for Prisoners is not part of the National Health Service (NHS) and prisoners do not have access to the normal NHS complaints procedures. Rather, the Prison Service aims to work in close relation to the NHS by contracting in NHS staff and services as appropriate. Each prison has a managing medical officer who arranges for a doctor to visit the prison every weekday.

Health care standards for the Prison Service state that

> The aim of the prison health care services (medical, nursing, pharmaceutical) is to provide for prisoners, to the extent that the constraints imposed by the prison environment and the facts of custody allow, a quality of care commensurate with that provided by the National Health Service for the general community, calling upon the specialist services of the NHS as necessary and appropriate.

However, prison medicine remains a separate and isolated arm of health care. In 1996, an inquiry into prison healthcare, conducted by HM Chief Inspector of Prisons, found that

> . . . although many health care staff in prisons can demonstrate an ever wider range of qualifications and flexibility in their work and working practices, the overall service provided, across the spectrum of establishments, does not match up to National Health standards, or satisfy the provisions of the *Patients' Charter*.

The chief inspector found that medical staff in prisons were not as well trained or as up to date with new medical techniques as were NHS staff. In particular, the level of care for prisoners with mental health problems was inadequate. The chief inspector proposed that the Prison Service should purchase a health care service from the NHS tailored to the specific needs of the prison environment. This would mean that:

> certain NHS Trusts will be asked to assume certain responsibilities, and to ensure that adequate provision for Prison Service needs is included in all resource allocation. Only in this way can consistency of delivery to

99

everyone in the community, in or out of prison be ensured. NHS standards apply before and after custodial sentences, so why not during?

Apart from the high levels of illness in prisons, there are basic differences between health care in prisons and health care in the community. In particular, there is the need to control infectious diseases in a confined area, to care for large numbers of prisoners with mental health problems (see *Chapter 4*), to support vulnerable prisoners who may be prone to suicide or self-injury and to provide treatment programmes for drug misusers.

Infectious diseases
As is the case in the community, viruses such as HIV and Hepatitis A, B and C may be spread in prison through the use of shared or dirty needles to inject drugs and through sexual contact. The prison environment is unique in the opportunities it presents for the progression of the HIV and hepatitis viruses.

There are a high number of intravenous drug users in prison. Needle exchange schemes or facilities to clean needles are often not available. Moreover, many prisoners have not received any form of drug treatment and so are not aware of the dangers of sharing needles.

Although, in theory, condoms are available, unprotected sexual activity in prison increases the danger of infection. It has been estimated that between ten and 20 per cent of long term prisoners may take part in homosexual activities at some stage during their sentences. Because many of these prisoners are heterosexual by preference, there is a chance that HIV and hepatitis may spread from prison to the wider community.

The Prison Service policy on AIDS and HIV aims to prevent the spread of infection, protect the health of prisoners and staff and provide care and support for infected prisoners. The strategy includes the medical treatment and counselling of known HIV patients as well as education of the general prison population on the ways to avoid infection. It also recognises that, because illegal activities such as drug misuse take place in prison, steps must be taken to minimise their harm. Therefore, governors have been advised to make available sterilising equipment for needles and syringes, and guidance on how to clean injecting equipment, although this often does not happen.

There is no mandatory test for HIV in prison, although tests are recommended for prisoners who are thought to be members of a 'high risk group'. Prisoners may also be tested at their own request. Prisoners who test positive are not normally segregated from the mainstream prison population, although if they are allocated a double cell, they share with another prisoner who has the HIV virus.

100

Suicide prevention
In recent years there has been a steady increase in the number of prisoners taking their own lives. Over the past twelve years (1986-1997), there has been a total of 577 self-inflicted deaths in prison and a threefold increase in the yearly average number of suicides. On average, a prisoner now commits suicide in prison once every five days.

During 1997, there were 70 self-inflicted deaths, most notably amongst young offenders, remand prisoners, mentally ill prisoners and life sentenced prisoners. Prisoners are between twice and seven times more likely to commit suicide than individuals within the general population. They are particularly at risk during the first few days in custody.

1986	1987	1988	1989	1990	1991	1992	1993	1994	1995	1996	1997
21	46	37	48	50	42	41	46	62	60	64	70

Recorded self-inflicted deaths in custody, England and Wales, 1986-97

In 1996, prisoners under the age of 21 comprised on average 13 per cent of the prison population. During that year, 14 (22 per cent) of the self-inflicted deaths involved prisoners under 21. Twenty six (41 per cent) of self-inflicted deaths occurred amongst prisoners aged 25 or under.

The Prison Service has attributed the sharp rise in the number of prison suicides to a rise in suicide amongst young men within the general population, as well as operational pressures and prison overcrowding. These conditions are most prominent in local prisons which is where the majority of suicides occur. Of all self-inflicted deaths between 1990 and 1996, no fewer than two-thirds occurred in local prisons.

Recent research has shown that prison suicides have multiple causes and motivations, including a history of anxiety or depression, stress from being bullied in prison and situational triggers, such as a change of location or a missed visit. The findings reveal inadequacies in the traditional view that suicide is an exclusively medical problem, a fact recognised by the 1989 Prison Service Circular Instruction, which has guided the development of Prison Service policy on suicide prevention ever since:

> In its widest sense, it [suicide prevention policy] must be about creating a climate in which suicidal thoughts and feelings are less likely to take root. Inmates will normally be less prone to resort to suicidal behaviour in the

101

establishment where regimes are full, varied and relevant; where staff morale is high and relationships with inmates positive; where good basic living conditions are provided; where every effort is made to encourage contacts with family and the community.

Current practice
In 1994 the Self Harm At Risk procedure was introduced into prisons, the overall aim of which is to 'enable a high quality of care to be given to prisoners who are identified as being at possible risk of self-harm or suicide'. To put the procedure into practice, guidelines have been developed for the primary care, special care and aftercare of prisoners who have been assessed as a suicide risk. Multi-disciplinary Suicide Awareness Teams have been charged with the responsibility of overseeing delivery of the procedures in each prison. Primary care involves the isolation of seriously at risk prisoners in separate cells so that they can be monitored regularly; special care and aftercare involves the support of prisoners through counselling. Suicide Awareness Teams are responsible for customising the procedures to the needs of individual prisons.

Drugs in prison
Given the rise in drug use amongst young people in recent years, it is perhaps not surprising that drugs are also widely available in prison and are an important part of the 'black market' economy. There is no precise information about the scale of drug misuse, although various studies suggest that about one-quarter of the prison population have a history of drug dependency and as many as 80 per cent have been regular users of alcohol and/or cannabis.

Research has estimated that around 20 per cent of sentenced adult males are dependent drug users (16 per cent of male sentenced young offenders and 29 per cent of sentenced females). In 1995, an Office of Population Censuses and Surveys study found that 62 per cent of prisoners had used illicit drugs prior to imprisonment, 82 per cent of whom were under the age of 21.

The relationship between drug use and crime—it has been estimated that half of the £34 billion cost of theft recorded by the police is attributable to drugs—concern about the spread of HIV and AIDS in prisons through the sharing of dirty needles, and a rise in the incidence of bullying and intimidation, in part arising from the fact that drugs are used as a major form of currency in prisons, has meant that reducing drug use has become a major strategic priority for the Prison Service in recent years.

In 1995, the Prison Service Drugs Strategy was launched to:

102

- reduce the supply of drugs;
- reduce the demand for drugs and rehabilitate drug users;
- reduce the potential for damage to the health of prisoners, staff and the wider community, arising from the misuse of drugs.

The strategy emphasises that

> the Prison Service will not tolerate the presence and use of illicit drugs in its establishments.

Prison governors have developed multi-disciplinary teams of prison officers, probation staff, health care staff, chaplains and drug agencies in the community who are responsible for monitoring the strategy and ensuring it strikes an appropriate balance between control and treatment.

Attempts to reduce the supply of drugs through enhanced security include the use of sniffer dogs, the searching of visitors, the installation of CCTV surveillance systems in visiting rooms and the increased use of non-contact and closed visits.

The control of drugs is also enforced by the use of Mandatory Drug Testing (MDT). MDT requires prisoners to provide a urine sample which is used to test for all the common drugs: opiates, LSD, Ecstasy, cocaine and cannabis. Prisoners are either selected at random or are targeted as likely drug users. Those who test positive, or refuse to take the test, are punished by fines, having privileges removed, or, most commonly, by having days added to their sentence.

Between February 1995 and January 1996, when MDT was initially piloted in a small number of prisons, a total of 3,075 prisoners either tested positive or refused to provide a sample. This resulted in prisoners receiving a total of 23,552 additional days. Between March 1996 and April 1997, the first year that MDT has operated on a national basis, 13,797 prisoners tested positively for illegal drugs. The most recent figures suggest that around 20 per cent of prisoners are testing positive. Actual drug use may be higher as some substances (notably opiates like heroin) can only be detected for a few days after they have been used. However, the trend does seem to be downward. In general, drug use is much lower in young offender institutions.

Drug treatment in prisons is mostly provided by community based agencies. No single treatment programme is advocated by the Prison Service and programmes vary from short drug awareness courses to therapeutic communities where prisoners can spend up to 18 months of their sentence undergoing intensive treatment. In addition, most newly admitted prisoners who have been assessed as being dependent on opiates by health care staff are put on a short Methadone detoxification programme (although some prison doctors refuse to prescribe Methadone).

Overall, the Prison Service Drugs Strategy has been criticised for failing to provide sufficient resources for drug treatment. To date there has been little evaluation of the effectiveness of drug treatment programmes and no national standards developed to govern their use. In comparison, over half of the £10 million plus that the Prison Service has spent on the control and treatment of drugs has been swallowed up by MDT. Not only is MDT expensive to operate, but because of the decision to punish drug offenders by imposing additional days on their sentence, indirectly it has also contributed to a significant rise in the prison population. In 1996, the additional days imposed as a punishment for the 21,000 drug related offences increased the prison population by about 500 extra prisoners per day, enough to fill an average prison.

MDT has also been criticised for influencing some prisoners to switch from cannabis to opiates because cannabis remains in the user's blood stream for much longer than opiates—28 days compared to three days. As testing is rarely carried out over the weekend, prisoners using opiates on a Friday night are likely to be clear in time for a Monday test. Research carried out by the Medical Research Council has found that the use of opiates increased from 4.1 per cent to 7.4 per cent during the first four months of the programme.

In May 1998, following a comprehensive review, the Prison Service revised the drugs strategy, while at the same time maintaining its basic aims of tackling the supply, demand and health consequences of drugs in prison. Amongst other things, the new strategy places a greater emphasis on voluntary testing, made possible by a decrease in the use of mandatory testing procedures. It recommends the use of a wider range of punishments, rather than relying on the imposition of additional days. It proposes the provision of more treatment programmes; and it aims to target those drugs which cause the most harm to prisoners and prisoner safety, the first indication that the Prison Service considers drugs to have different levels of seriousness.

Sex in prison

Prisoners in England and Wales are not allowed conjugal visits. This means that sexual contact between prisoners and their partners during visits is prohibited (although it sometimes occurs).

The Sexual Offences Act 1967 prohibits sex between men except that which occurs in a private place between two consenting adults aged 18 or over. Confusion over whether a prison cell constitutes a private place has never been satisfactorily resolved. A letter to prison health care managers from Dr. Rosemary Wool, then director of health care for the Prison Service, suggested that consenting acts between adult prisoners

> are not automatically unlawful and that a prison cell is in many circumstances capable of being deemed a private place under the terms of the 1967 Sexual Offences Act . . . there may be a legal risk in not providing condoms in the relevant set of circumstances through a failure in the duty of care.

Dr. Wool encouraged prison doctors to prescribe condoms

> when in their clinical judgement there is a known risk of HIV infection as a result of HIV risk sexual behaviour.

However, the method of distribution recommended by the Prison Service AIDS Advisory Committee and supported by the National Aids and Prisons Forum—that condoms should be placed 'in open containers in reception, the health care centre and other locations where potential users have the opportunity to take them unobserved'—has not been implemented.

CHAPTER 6

Prison Regimes

The various day-to-day routines and activities in prisons constitute what is commonly known as the prison regime. Routines include the times during the day that prisoners wake up, have breakfast, work, have lunch, have tea, exercise, go to sleep etc.

Activities include the means by which prisoners are kept occupied during the day. Activities in prisons are divided broadly into work, education, P.E. and offence related programmes. Work, education and P.E. aim to provide prisoners with a range of life and social skills, whereas offence related programmes aim to tackle prisoners' offending behaviour.

Prison regimes therefore include everything that affects prisoners during their period in custody: security, control and safety, race relations, hygiene, food, clothing, accommodation, reception, discharge and transfer, request and complaint procedures, legal matters, religion, health services, welfare, visits, work, education, offence related programmes, throughcare, etc.

Some regime activities are subject to minimum standards, although frequently these are open-ended and unenforceable. For example, Prison Rule 27A entitles prisoners not engaged in outdoor work, or detained in open prisons 'to spend time in the open air at least once a day, for such period as may be reasonable in the circumstances'. The Prison Service is also committed to providing prisoners with at least seven hours of constructive regime activity per day. However, the quality of regimes can vary considerably according to the security category and status of the prison and the facilities available.

All convicted prisoners in training prisons are required to work or attend training, education or offence related programmes. Unconvicted prisoners are not required to work but are encouraged to do so. Under Prison Rule 20, unconvicted prisoners are entitled to wear their own clothes. A major part of the regime in a local prison is the induction of prisoners into life inside the prison system. Open prisons perform the opposite function. Because, for the most part, they accommodate prisoners who have already been through the prison system and are nearing release, open prisons organize routines and activities which aim to prepare prisoners for life outside prison.

The following is adapted from the midweek routine for prisoners at Preston prison, a busy local prison, originally built in 1790 and re-built and enlarged in the mid-Victorian period. The routine provides details of a typical day in the life of a prisoner in a local prison.

0630	Caterer on duty.
0700	Early staff on duty.
0745	Main staff on duty. Cells are unlocked. Breakfast is taken. Applications to see the governor, probation officer, doctor etc. are made.
0830	Prisoners go to work or attend education.
0900	Special visits. Prisoners queue for the doctor. Exercise period.
1100	Visits end.
1110	Prisoners take lunch.
1215	Roll check. Prisoners locked in cells while main staff take lunch.
1315	Main staff return from lunch. Visits re-commence.
1330	Prisoners return to work or attend education. Exercise period.
1345	Unconvicted prisoners are allowed association period.
1350	Punishment exercise commences.
1530	Visits end.
1600	Prisoners take tea.
1700	Roll check. Main staff leave prison.
1730	Prisoners unlocked for education, gymnasium, chapel, association.
2000	Association finishes.
2045	Night staff on duty.
2100	Evening patrol staff on duty.

THE DEVELOPMENT OF REGIMES

Routines and activities in prison help to maintain order. Well organized and active prisons are safe prisons. Prisoners who are encouraged to make the best possible use of their time by engaging in activities are less likely to cause trouble for prison staff. This principle, which underpins the development of safe prisons, is sometimes referred to as 'dynamic security'.

Fundamental to the principle of 'dynamic security' is the development of good quality staff/prisoner relationships. Security is not regarded as separate from the daily interactions between staff and prisoners, but instead is an integral part of all activities in prisons. Prisoners are less motivated to escape or cause control problems if they feel safe from assault from other prisoners and if they have trust and confidence in prison staff. They are also less likely to cause disturbances if they are occupied in meaningful activities for large parts of the day.

However, Prison Rule 1, which states that: 'The purpose of the training and treatment of convicted prisoners shall be to encourage and assist them to lead a good and useful life' suggests that activities in prisons are not only provided for the purpose of keeping prisoners occupied, but also to rehabilitate and prepare them for release as law abiding citizens.

The development of good quality regimes is therefore bound up with the debate about the overall purpose of prisons which was discussed in *Chapter 1*. Efforts to develop programmes which aim to rehabilitate offenders have been affected by disagreement over what prisons are for and about the underlying factors which may influence offending behaviour.

But differing views about the causes of crime are not the only factor to have influenced the development of prison regimes. The findings of academic research into 'what works' with prisoners have also had a significant impact.

For many years, the most influential piece of academic research was a review published in America in 1974 by a researcher called Robert Martinson. His paper, *What Works? Questions and Answers About Prison Reform*, argued that 'rehabilitative efforts that have been reported so far have had no appreciable effect on recidivism'. And his conclusion that 'nothing works' in prison to influence offenders away from a life of crime had a profoundly damaging impact on the development of prison regimes.

Today, the findings of Martinson's survey have been largely discredited. The survey reviewed 231 studies of the effectiveness of community and penal sanctions reported between 1945 and 1967. The methodology involved an aggregation of 231 studies, which were presented as a brief summary statement of whether rehabilitation programmes worked or not. By employing re-conviction rates as a measure only, and by not reviewing each study separately, no account was taken of whether prisoners were re-convicted of different offences or whether re-conviction was the consequence of any additional factors beyond the sphere of influence of the various programmes. The methodology also failed to take account of how prison sentences, in different prisons, can vary in the way they are delivered and, therefore, of the effects this may have had, on the final results.

However, at the time, Martinson's work was accepted as proof that rehabilitative programmes for offenders were a waste of time and money. Subsequently, Martinson reversed his position although this was little reported. 'Nothing works' seemed to chime with political philosophies on both the Neo-conservative Right and the Radical Left.

Subsequent studies to Martinson have demonstrated the impact of well-designed and well-implemented programmes on high risk sexual and violent offenders. In addition, the influence of education and employment on lower risk offenders has became more widely accepted.

The word 'regime' is perhaps an unfortunate one. As a 1984 Prison Service Report, *Managing the Long Term Prison System: Report of the Control Review Committee*, stated:

> The concept of the regime is large and vague, and implies generally that every prisoner in an establishment is subject to the same process regardless of his needs or abilities.

In order to convey the idea that activities in prison are customised to the needs of individual prisoners and are amenable to review, the Committee suggested that the phrase 'regime activities' should be replaced with 'prisoner programmes'.

Although, many of the components which comprise quality regimes apply to all kinds of prisons and to all kinds of prisoners, there is now greater recognition that prison regimes should reflect the needs and abilities of the individual prisoners contained within them. Today, it is widely accepted that a major objective of work, education and offence related programmes is to tackle the underlying offending behaviour which caused offenders to end up in prison in the first place.

Significant progress has been made in recent years. The Prison Service is now committed to unlocking prisoners for at least 12 hours per day, seven hours of which should be to engage in so called 'purposeful activities'. Key performance indicators have been devised which include targets for the number of prisoners who complete accredited offending behaviour programmes. Differential or incentive based regimes have been developed which are supposed to reward prisoners for good behaviour and try to influence them to make the best use of their time in custody. In many ways, such programmes complement systems of early release, such as remission and parole, which are intended—in part—to act as an incentive for prisoners to behave and to make progress during their sentences.

RELEASE ON LICENCE

The early release of prisoners has been used to try to influence prisoner behaviour since 1898, when a system of remission was introduced which allowed prisoners the opportunity to earn time off their sentence. In 1921, the Head of the Prison Commission, Sir Evelyn Ruggles-Brise commented that

. . . the risk or fear of losing remission marks operates as a powerful deterrent against idleness or misconduct and it has been found, generally, that under the influence of this salutary provision, there has been a marked improvement in the tone and demeanour of the prisoners, while, at the same time, an aid has been furnished to those responsible for maintaining order and discipline.

Another form of early release, parole, differed from remission in that it was discretionary, rather than an automatic entitlement. Parole was introduced by the Criminal Justice Act 1967 after its use was justified in the government White Paper, *The Adult Offender*, 1965:

A considerable number of long term prisoners reach a recognisable peak in their training at which they may respond to generous treatment, but after which, if kept in prison, they may go downhill.

Although the idea of a 'peak in their training' is now regarded as mistaken, research showing that release on supervision can reduce the risk of an offender returning to crime informed the development of a new sentencing system introduced in 1991. This now requires prisoners to serve part of their sentence in prison and part in the community under the supervision of the probation service. The reasoning behind the new approach was spelled out in the White Paper, *Crime, Justice and Protecting the Public*, 1990:

. . . there is no longer justification for arrangements for the discretionary early release of prisoners sentenced to short sentences, but there are benefits in a form of early release which combines encouragement to good behaviour in prison with an incentive to avoid re-offending on release. The aim of preventing re-offending can be buttressed by a period of compulsory supervision on release and a liability to be returned to custody if convicted of further imprisonable offences before the original sentence imposed by the court has expired.

As such, remission and parole no longer exist. However, the words remain in common parlance. Indeed, the Parole Board remains in existence and long-term prisoners are informed of their non-parole date (NPD), i.e. the latest day on which they will be released, assuming they do not breach prison discipline during their sentence.

The current structure, which formed part of the Criminal Justice Act 1991, entitles prisoners serving sentences of under four years to Automatic Conditional Release (ACR) on supervision at the halfway point of their sentence, unless they incur 'additional days' as a disciplinary punishment. Prisoners serving four years and above become eligible for release on licence to the probation service at the half-

110

way point (although this is not automatic) and are anyway released at the two-thirds point of their sentence, unless they incur 'additional days'. This system of Discretionary Conditional Release (DCR) involves an assessment of individual cases by the Parole Board. The Board can release prisoners serving up to seven years; in the case of prisoners serving still longer sentences, the home secretary has the final say. Prisoners remain on licence until the threequarters point of their sentence and, if they commit a further offence, are 'at risk' of serving the remainder of their sentence to the 100 per cent point.

The Parole Board also considers whether ACR and DCR prisoners have breached the terms of their supervision licence and should be returned to prison. The board is comprised of professional and lay people including judges, psychiatrists, criminologists and probation officers. Some ACR prisoners may also be recalled to prison by the sentencing court which has the power to suspend supervision licences for a period of up to six months.

There are slightly different arrangements of release on licence for certain groups of prisoners. For instance, prisoners serving less than 12 months are not subject to supervision on release, unless the offender specifically requests it. Young offenders serving less than 12 months are subject to three months supervision, provided this does not take them beyond their twenty second birthday. Prisoners serving long sentences for sexual or violent offences may be subject to an extended period of post-release supervision if the court considers this necessary to protect the public. All life sentenced prisoners are subject to supervision on licence indefinitely, except when the Parole Board decides this would no longer serve a useful purpose.

Finally, as part of the Crime and Disorder Act 1998, a new system of home detention curfew (electronic tagging) is to be introduced at the beginning of 1999 for prisoners serving between three months and four years. Under this scheme, prisoners who have been assessed as suitable, will be released up to two months early subject to their being tagged and subject to curfew for at least nine hours a day.

Tagged prisoners are released on licence for supervision in the community by the Probation Service. If further offences are committed while under supervision, or they are otherwise in breach of their licence, offenders are recalled or returned to prison as described above.

DIFFERENTIAL REGIMES

The Incentives and Earned Privileges scheme was introduced across the prison system during 1995. The scheme aims to encourage responsible behaviour, hard work and to create a more disciplined, better controlled and safer environment for prisoners and staff. It includes the following privileges, awarded to prisoners who demonstrate good behaviour and a willingness to cooperate:

- access to private cash above set minima
- extra or improved visits
- eligibility to participate in enhanced earning schemes
- earned community visits
- own clothes
- time out of cell for association.

The framework involves a three tier regime system: basic, standard and enhanced. The following table indicates the level of privilege that can be expected by prisoners on each level of the regime:

	Basic	Standard	Enhanced
Private cash	£2.50	£10	£15
Visits	1 hr per week	3 hrs per week	As standard
Enhanced earnings	No	No	Eligible
Community visits	No	No	Eligible
Own clothes	No	Yes	Yes
Association	9 hrs per week	12 hrs per week	14 hrs per week

The degree to which differential regimes have contributed to encouraging prisoners to conform and make better use of their time in custody is the subject of ongoing research and evaluation. Most staff regard the system as a useful addition to their powers. Most prisoners are more sceptical—pointing out that the incentives are either trivial or not available at all. There has also been criticism that the withdrawal of privileges like visiting entitlements punishes the prisoner's family as well as the prisoner.

MODEL REGIMES

Life sentenced prisoners
All life sentenced prisoners are managed centrally by a special unit within Prison Service headquarters. After being sentenced they are sent

to one of three Lifer Main Centres at Gartree in Leicestershire, Wormwood Scrubs or Wakefield, where a sentence plan is prepared which details how they can make the best use of their time while in custody and prepare for their release.

Internal Review Boards assess the progress of life sentenced prisoners on a regular basis and reports, which describe their behaviour, their attitude towards their offences, family matters etc., are sent to the Home Office once every three years. Such reports are used to assess the suitability of lifers to be re-categorised and sent to lower security or open prisons where they can more easily prepare for their release. In each prison a lifer liaison officer is responsible for monitoring the behaviour of lifers and contributing to assessments of their progress.

Remand prisoners

Following the Woolf Report, a separate Statement of Purpose reflecting the unique status of remand prisoners was drawn up by the Prison Service which included the delivery of 'opportunities for education, religious observance, exercise and recreation and, where possible, for training and work'.

In 1992, a *Model Regime for Local Prisons and Remand Centres* was published to provide a blueprint for planning

> high quality regimes at new establishments with modern facilities and for developing enhanced regimes at existing establishments as physical conditions are gradually improved and overcrowding is reduced.

The model regime includes the provision of a bail and a legal aid team to assist unconvicted prisoners to apply for bail and obtain legal representation, a range of work activities for both convicted and unconvicted prisoners, and information at induction and throughout the period in custody on issues affecting prisoners in local gaols.

However, despite efforts to raise standards, the implementation of model regimes for remand prisoners has been impeded in recent years by overcrowding, restrictions on prison expenditure and a deterioration in prison conditions. Local prisons, most of which date from Victorian times, have found it increasingly difficult to improve the quality of regimes as a result.

Women prisoners

In 1991, the Prison Service published *Regimes for Women*. The guidance recognised that women are convicted of far fewer serious crimes than men; that many have been the victims of sexual abuse; that some, though not all, have problems of low self-esteem and self-confidence;

and that many are mothers who will be separated from their children during the period of their imprisonment. The guidance recommended that women 'should not be subject to more restrictions (or searches) than are necessary for the purposes of security or good order or discipline'; that 'staff need to be aware of, and sympathetic to the very natural worries to which women will be subject'; that 'the use of temporary release for purposes of work, education or training is well established but offers scope for expansion'; and that 'governors should ensure that all women are told of the possibility of having their baby with them in a mother and baby unit'.

But as has been the case with local prisons, little progress has been made. In particular, the escape of nine high security male prisoners from Whitemoor and Parkhurst prisons in 1995 resulted in restrictions on women prisoners to attend work or education in the community and visit their families at home.

In December 1995, the female prison estate became the subject of close media attention when HM Chief Inspector of Prisons abandoned an inspection of Holloway prison because of the 'totally unacceptable conditions for both prisoners and staff' he found there. As we have seen, there was also widespread public disquiet over the imposition of new security measures which resulted in the shackling of pregnant women prisoners in hospital right up to the point of giving birth.

For these and other reasons, a thematic review of *Women in Prison*, undertaken by HM Chief Inspector of Prisons in May 1997, recommended that

> the women's prison system ought to be managed, as an entity, by one director, with responsibility and accountability for all that happens within the women's estate.

An underlying reason for the recommendation was to

> encourage the Prison Service to make better arrangements for the separate management of the fast-rising numbers of women in prison, and to provide regimes appropriate to their needs, not merely to adapt those designed for men.

As mentioned in *Chapter 3*, this was approved partially when an assistant director for women prisoners, supported by a Women's Policy Group, responsible for the development of model regimes for women prisoners, was appointed at the beginning of 1998.

Young offenders
HM Chief Inspector of Prisons has also recommended that the young offender estate is managed separately. Two inspection reports of young

offender institutions at Onley in Warwickshire and Dover in Kent, published in early 1997, as well as an uncompleted inspection of Glen Parva in Leicestershire, raised grave concerns about the quality of regimes in YOIs, and the level of bullying found there.

Yet not all YOIs have received bad reports. Lancaster Farms has been highly praised by both HM Chief Inspector and the Prison Reform Trust as providing a high quality regime for young offenders. The aim and motto of Lancaster Farms is to 'Prevent the Next Victim' and all aspects of the regime are directed towards encouraging young offenders to lead crime free lives in future. The regime is based on the development of positive relationships between prisoners and staff and incorporates a 'Nature of Adolescence: Working with Young People in Custody' training package, devised by the Trust for the Study of Adolescence (TSA). The package has been designed to enable prison staff to uncover specific reasons for adolescent offending and to become aware of how to prepare young people for adulthood. TSA has since introduced the package into 20 YOIs and over 2,000 staff have completed the course.

However, the quality of regimes for young offenders is very variable. In *Young Prisoners: A Thematic Review* (October 1997), HM Chief Inspector of Prisons criticised the lack of strategic thinking regarding the development of regimes for young offenders:

> With the demise of borstal training it has become unfashionable to engage in serious debate about appropriate regimes for young people, and there are few, if any, incentives for managers in the Prison Service to want to specialise in this area of work.

The chief inspector's solution was to recommend that children (under 18) should be removed entirely from Prison Service custody and that young adults (18-20) should be separately managed by a Director of Young Prisoners. He said that regimes for young offenders should include three basic elements: intensive induction, including a thinking skills course; a training and employment scheme, including job search; and a pre-release course, including help with finding suitable accommodation. As was the case with women, an assistant director, responsible for the development of regimes for young offenders was created at the beginning of 1998.

COMPONENTS OF REGIMES

Reception
Prisoners admitted to local prisons for the first time go through a reception process in which personal details, such as their religious

denomination and any items of personal property they have brought into the prison, are recorded. All prisoners are given a prison number which remains the same throughout their sentence and through any subsequent moves to other prisons. All prisoners also undergo a medical examination.

Many prisoners who are experiencing prison life for the first time are likely to be apprehensive about what lies in store for them. Therefore, an assessment is made of their mental health, their perceived ability to cope with prison life and whether they present any possible risk of suicide. Prisoners who are assessed as being vulnerable to suicide should receive additional support in the form of counselling. In an attempt to reduce fears, the reception process provides basic information about the routine for the first night in prison. Telephones should be made available in the reception area. Prisoners are allowed one call to relatives or friends and one call to a legal adviser at the public's expense.

As soon as possible after reception, all prisoners are required to take a bath or shower. At the end of the reception process, prisoners are allocated cells and necessary kit is provided, such as razor blades, soap etc. A card on the door of the cell gives the name of the prisoner, their prison number, length of sentence and religion. Importantly, it does not mention their offence, so other prisoners need not know what they have done.

Induction

Induction should begin on the first morning and may take up to a week to complete. Information about the Prison Rules is provided and each prisoner should be issued with a copy of the *Prisoner's Information Book,* which answers basic questions about imprisonment. More detailed information is provided in meetings with the governor, the chaplain, the Probation Department, the Education Department, the Work Allocation Board and the Board of Visitors. As well as providing information to prisoners, the induction process should also assess any housing or family responsibilities they may have and their employment and education needs.

Allocation

Once they have been sentenced, prisoners normally return from court to a local prison to await allocation to a training prison. Allocation depends on the length of sentence to be served and the prisoner's security categorisation. It also depends on which prisons have space available. Prisoners serving very short sentences tend to remain in local prisons.

Sentence planning

Sentence planning is the process which is supposed to ensure prisoners are helped to lead 'law-abiding and useful lives in custody and after release'. The purpose of sentence planning is set out, somewhat inelegantly, in the Prison Service *Annual Report* for 1992/93:

> Sentence planning underpins all of the Prison Service's goals. It aims to make the best use of the time people have to spend in custody, to reduce the risk of their re-offending and to help them to lead law-abiding and useful lives in custody and after release. It links work on helping prisoners to tackle their offending behaviour with planned experience of work, training and education. It provides opportunities to review the prisoner's progress throughout the sentence. It is also the mechanism for co-ordinating work done in prison with work done with prisoners who will have a period of compulsory supervision after release.

In other words, sentence planning aims to provide both prisoners and staff with clear guidance on the programmes and activities most suitable to an individual prisoner's needs. Needs are assessed in relation to the range of opportunities offered within and outside of prisons, including work, education, vocational training, offence-related programmes, links with the community and pre-release and development courses.

Sentence planning has its origins in the practice of allocating life sentence prisoners to training and work activities according to individual need. But it was not until 1989 that a formal system of sentence planning was introduced for young offenders, prisoners serving over 10 years and sex offenders. It was extended to other prisoners two years later because the parole and supervision requirements of the Criminal Justice Act 1991 demanded consistency in the way in which the progress of prisoners through their sentences was assessed and recorded. Sentence planning began in October 1992 for prisoners sentenced to over four years and in October 1993 for prisoners sentenced to over 12 months.

Because the sentencing arrangements introduced by the Criminal Justice Act 1991, incorporate both custodial and community based elements, an essential function of sentence planning is to provide a mechanism for the prison and probation services to work together. The aim is for the sentence plan to take account of both the custodial and supervisory components of the sentence and to reflect the contribution which each service can make to encouraging offenders to live crime free lives in the future.

117

The *National Framework for the Throughcare of Offenders in Custody to the Completion of Supervision in the Community* (1993) describes throughcare as follows:

> The term throughcare embraces all the assistance given to offenders and their families by the Prison and Probation Services and outside agencies and ties in with all the training, education and work experience they are given. It is directed at equipping them to fit back into society, get a job and home and cope with life without offending. It includes all the support and help which is given to unconvicted prisoners and their families by the Prison and Probation Services and outside agencies.

Each prison seconds probation officers from the local probation service for between three and five years, for which they are paid slightly higher rates of pay than probation officers in the community. Depending on the size and status of the prison, throughcare services may include all or part of the following:

- group work;
- individual work, including sentence planning and risk assessments;
- specialist work;
- partnership work with external organizations.

Group work involves probation officers leading groups of prisoners in offence related subjects such as general offending behaviour, victims issues, drug misuse, anger management and car crime. Social skills, such as parenting, thinking skills and money management are also addressed.

Individual work involves probation officers working on a one-to-one basis with prisoners on the preparation and implementation of sentence plans. All prisoners serving one year or more are allocated a 'home probation officer' who ultimately is responsible for supervising the prisoner once they have been released on licence. The home probation officer maintains contact with the prisoner on a regular basis to ensure that relevant information about the prisoner's home circumstances are taken into account and that the prisoner's sentence plan is properly focused.

Prison probation officers also help convicted prisoners with specific problems related to their sentence and advise remand prisoners about bail rights, housing, benefit entitlements, child care and other practical matters.

A joint report by the Prison Service and the Probation Service, *Report of the Review of Sentence Planning* (1995) found that, although the theory behind sentence planning is a sound one, in practice there are major structural problems with the way it has been implemented. The report found that sentence planning is the: 'first task which gets dropped when there is pressure', that there are 'considerable gaps in knowledge and understanding about the operation and purpose of sentence planning at all levels', and that 'a great deal still needs to be done to achieve the effective working relationships between the Prison and Probation Services on which sentence planning depends'.

In order to improve these working relationships, in July 1997, the new home secretary, Jack Straw, announced that a review to identify the options for better and closer integration between the two services would be conducted at ministerial level by Joyce Quin, the minister then responsible for both the prison and probation services.

Risk assessments
Probation officers also make a major contribution to assessing the risk which prisoners might pose if granted parole or release on temporary licence. The Probation Service National Standards state the following:

> In every case an assessment of the risk posed by the offender should be made. This should consider the risk to the public of re-offending or of causing serious harm (and its likely nature). Assessments should also consider the risk of suicide or self-harm and risk to staff.

> Risk assessment is not a one-off activity; it should commence as soon as the offender is received into custody and then be undertaken systematically at regular intervals so that any changes in circumstances or specific new problems arising are noted and appropriate action taken. Assessment of risk is particularly important when considering early release on temporary licence or recall.

Home probation officers also make assessments of the prisoner's home circumstances by visiting the family or other release address. In cases involving serious sexual and other violent offences, home probation officers should arrange for the victim or the victim's family to be contacted within two months of sentence and offered the opportunity to express any concerns they may have when the offender's release is considered.

Work and training
Under Prison Rule 28(1) work is compulsory for all convicted prisoners. The Rule states:

A convicted prisoner shall be required to do useful work for not more than ten hours a day, and arrangements shall be made to allow prisoners to work, where possible, outside the cells and in association with one another.

Unconvicted prisoners may work if they choose to do so.

Until the end of the last century, prison work was perceived primarily as a punishment and was characterised by hard, monotonous labour. Such labour was often deliberately purposeless, as with the notorious crank and treadmill. Work as punishment was abolished officially in 1898. However, progress has been slow in improving the quality of activity available in prisons. For example, in 1951, the House of Commons Select Committee on Estimates found that 'a considerable proportion of the work done [in prisons] is routine work of a monotonous nature'. The committee recommended that the introduction of vocational training would improve the quality of work available. The committee argued that:

> The mind of a man is just as likely to stand still as the waves of the sea. If he is to spend five or ten years in prison, the cramped conditions in which mind and body exercise will inevitably disturb his proper perspective on life. He will indulge in self-pity, he will magnify trifles, he will grow more anti-social. This can be checked and developed by a continuous course of study. If he does not think at all for five or ten years, but merely moves his hands in the workshop, and taxes his digestive organs three times a day, his time in prison will be a period of stagnation and may well result in a sort of mental paralysis. If he is cursed with an active or inquisitive mind and is not provided with the means of exercising it along healthy channels, his mind will not stagnate but get poisoned by self-pity, and he will emerge even more anti-social than he was before.

Prior to the nationalisation of prisons in 1878, work was often organized for the private profit of the gaolers. Today, the majority of work activities in prisons are organized to meet the serviceable needs of the prison system. The Prison Service maintains its own buildings and does most of its own washing, cooking and cleaning. Textile workshops produce clothing for prisoners and uniforms for staff. Engineering and woodwork shops produce security grilles and various items of prison furniture. The produce from prison farms is consumed almost entirely within the prison system. A small amount of contract work undertaken for outside customers includes unskilled and low-skill packaging, processing and assembly activities. In addition, a small number of prisons have sub-contracted with private companies who manage prison workshops for commercial profit.

Because it is not subject to commercial timescales, most prison work is generally slower and working hours are generally shorter than work in the community. The working day is generally restricted to the five hours between 9.15 a.m. and 11.45 a.m., and 1.30 p.m. and 4 p.m. because of the times at which meals are taken. It is also subject to frequent interruptions to allow prisoners to attend other activities, such as exercise periods, visits to the library etc.

Vocational training is workshop based, with the exception of courses in information technology, which form part of the education curriculum and are usually taught in classrooms. Training in traditionally male, manual activities, such as engineering, construction industry training and woodwork, predominates. Attempts to improve the standard of training in prisons have resulted in an increase in the number of prisoners gaining recognised vocational qualifications. In 1994-95 a total of 13,475 National Vocational Qualifications (NVQs) were awarded to prisoners in 48 different trades and occupations. However, much prison based training remains irrelevant to the changing labour market outside of prisons. A rare counter example is industrial cleaning, courses in which are offered in many prisons.

According to its Statement of Purpose, Prison Enterprise Services (the department within the Prison Service responsible for providing work and training) is

> committed to serving and supporting prison establishments in the cost-effective provision of purposeful work and training, thereby giving prisoners the opportunity to acquire knowledge, attitudes, skills and habits which will help them to lead law abiding and useful lives in custody and after release.

The problem with the statement is that it does not follow that work necessary to service and maintain prisons also provides prisoners with the skills necessary to compete for jobs after release. Questions about the purpose of prison work remain. Is the primary purpose of work and training to maintain the prison system? Is it for industrial production? Is it to give prisoners something to do? Is it to provide vocational training and to help prisoners obtain employment after release? Or is it intended to be all these things?

The Woolf Report argued that work is central to a 'planned programme for prisoner development'. In particular:

> prisons should draw up plans to reach a situation in which the hours of work correspond closely to those in the world outside the prison;

> education, training and work should be brought together to provide the most constructive mix to assist prisoners after release;

> there should be a greater diversity of types of work in prisons, to encompass the involvement of other employers and cooperation with local

121

Training and Enterprise Councils, and also to allow prisoners to improve their self-esteem by making goods for charitable causes;

responsibility for the provision of the most appropriate mix of education, training and work in prisons should be re-allocated to the individual prison governor.

However, despite the fact that the White Paper, *Custody, Care and Justice*, supported Woolf's recommendations for improvements in work and training, little progress has been made. There remains a serious imbalance between the jobs on offer in prison and those available in the community. For the most part, proposals that prisons should develop closer links with Training and Enterprise Councils (TECs), the bodies responsible for customising vocational training in the community to the future requirements of the labour market, have not been acted upon. Work in declining industrial areas such as mechanical engineering and textiles remain irrelevant to the expanding service sector jobs in hotel and catering, business services, leisure etc. And because the majority of prisoners come from urban areas, work experience on farms and in gardens is of little practical use to them. Indeed, most prison farms are very inefficient; in agriculture proper, machinery has replaced farm labour.

Apart from the lack of certainty about what work in prisons is for, attempts to improve the quality of prison based work and training have been constrained by other organizational priorities—in particular, the primary need of the Prison Service to accommodate securely an increasing number of prisoners. Work and training in prisons is also hampered by the short working day, the inability of prisoners serving short sentences to benefit from work experience or training and the frequent transfer of prisoners to other prisons because of the pressures of overcrowding.

Education

Under Circular Instruction 40/88, young offenders must receive two hours of education per week and prisoners under 16 years of age must be provided with at least 15 hours education or training per week. There are no formal obligations on prisons to provide education for adults. However, Prison Rule 29 states:

1. Every prisoner able to profit from the education facilities provided at a prison shall be encouraged to do so.

Programmes of evening educational classes shall be arranged at every prison and, subject to any directions of the secretary of state, reasonable facilities shall be afforded to prisoners who wish to do so to improve their education by correspondence courses or private study, or to practice handicrafts, in their spare time.

Special attention shall be paid to the education of illiterate prisoners, and if necessary they shall be taught within the hours normally allotted to work.

Prior to the Prison Act 1877, education in prisons was the responsibility of the prison chaplain and consisted mostly of religious instruction and Bible reading. Unlike work, education in prisons was introduced for the purpose of occupying prisoners, not punishing them. Not everyone approved. In 1885, the chairman of the Prison Commission, Sir Edmund Du Cane, wrote of Reading Gaol:

> In this prison the inmates learned lessons all day, except when exercising, attending chapel and cleaning cells, etc. As a privilege they might, when tired of reading, pick a little oakum, but this was quite optional, and hard, heavy labour was absolutely forbidden in order that the whole attention might be devoted to literature — the establishment was a criminal university, and acquired the name of the 'Read-Read-Reading Gaol'.

Gradually, the role of education has developed to become an increasingly important part of prison regimes. In 1919, notebooks and pencils were issued to prisoners for the first time, and in 1922 adult education classes taught by volunteers were introduced. In 1948, education in prisons became the responsibility of local education authorities; and on three separate occasions during the 1980s and early 1990s the House of Commons Education, Science and Arts Committee recommended the introduction of a Prison Regimes Act, which would more precisely define the role of education and introduce minimum standards of delivery.

The Woolf Report commented on the traditionally inferior place occupied by education within prisons and identified an uneven spread of classes across the prison system, long waiting lists, a lack of appropriate classroom facilities and classes frequently cancelled due to a lack of prison officers to provide escorts and security. The Woolf Report concluded that 'the argument in favour of extending educational opportunities as far as resources will allow is overwhelming'. It recommended that

> the Prison Service should make greater use of modular education courses, particularly for remand prisoners;

> education and work should be given equal standing within prison activities;

both prison officers and prisoners themselves should be more involved in the development of education programmes.

However, the then government dismissed calls for a Prison Regimes Act as 'neither necessary or desirable' and it contracted education in prisons out of the control of local education authorities by a process of compulsory competitive tendering. New contractors, it was argued, would introduce fresh ideas and encourage the innovation necessary to bring about increased efficiency and greater value for money.

The speed of this change, which resulted in the awarding of 47 new contracts for the delivery of education in 1993, was roundly criticised for causing confusion and uncertainty amongst prison teaching staff. Since then, cuts in the education budget—expenditure on prisoner education was reduced from £36,956,000 in 1995-1996 to £34,481,000 in 1996-1997—and the development of a new core curriculum, which has been paired down to consist of numeracy and literacy, information technology and life and social skills, has provoked further criticism. However, plans now being made by the Prison Service suggest a significant increase in educational opportunities in prisons may take place in the future.

Arts activities
Accounts of prisoners 'finding themselves' through the arts are common. Jimmy Boyle, who became an internationally renowned sculptor and author, and John McVicar, who became a successful journalist, are perhaps the best known, but there are many others. Drama, creative writing, painting and music are all available, although the quantity and quality varies considerably from prison to prison.

Arts activities are more concerned with internal goals—development of the 'self', communicating, respect—than with external goals—gaining qualifications, or skills directly applicable to employment. Because progress cannot be demonstrated as easily as with examination results and achievements are more subtle and more difficult to put into words, a condescending attitude towards prison arts activities has been expressed in some popular newspapers and by some prison officers.

However, there have been many positive outcomes stemming from prisoner involvement in arts activities. The Koestler Award Trust, which awards prizes for creative work produced by prisoners, was begun by the author and campaigner Arthur Koestler in 1962. (Koestler had himself been a prisoner, under sentence of death, during the Spanish Civil War). Since then it has grown to encompass 43 different categories of creative endeavour and culminates in an annual exhibition. Also, the Writers in Residence in Prisons Scheme, which aims to develop the writing skills of prisoners, was introduced in 1992 and has since influenced prisoners to produce a burgeoning number of prison magazines.

Offence-related programmes

All activities in prison are meant to encourage prisoners to lead crime free lives in future. However, there are a small number of programmes which seek either to tackle the causes of offending directly, or are aimed at factors which can contribute to offending, such as drug abuse.

Offence related programmes are delivered by psychologists, probation officers and specially trained prison officers. They include courses in three core areas: Thinking Skills, Reasoning and Rehabilitation and the Sex Offender Treatment Programme. Programmes which seek to challenge the behaviour of violent offenders are also currently being piloted. All offence related programmes in prisons are currently the subject of extensive evaluation.

Cognitive skills

Courses in Thinking Skills and Reasoning and Rehabilitation— sometimes referred to as cognitive skills programmes—normally take place in group sessions and include various cognitive exercises, games and role-play. Such courses developed from research which has shown that offenders demonstrate persistent deficits in their thinking compared to the general population. In general terms, offenders are more prone to the need to experience immediate gratification, to lead a life full of excitement, risks and thrills and to resort to simple and easy solutions to complex problems.

Offenders smoke more, experiment with drugs more, have earlier sexual experiences, are more promiscuous, fight more, gamble more, truant from school more and absent themselves from work more.

Research using cohorts of children followed over long periods of time has shown that criminal behaviour is also associated with a variety of social and psychological problems, including drug taking, alcohol abuse, school failure, unemployment and poor relationships. Childhood factors such as hyperactivity, impulsivity, attention deficit, family criminality, school failure and economic deprivation have also been linked to future criminal activity.

An important part of reducing the chance of re-offending is to make prisoners understand how crimes affect victims. It may seem axiomatic to many of us that there is no such thing as a victimless crime, but many offenders do not understand how crimes frequently cause great distress and anxiety to their victims. Indirectly, all offence related programmes attempt to challenge the attitudes of prisoners towards their victims.

125

But a small number of programmes have also been developed which address victims' issues more specifically, such as the provision of services by selected groups of prisoners in open prisons to local victim support groups.

The Sex Offender Treatment Programme

The Sex Offender Treatment Programme was introduced into prisons in 1991. It involves an initial assessment, which identifies each offender's treatment needs and includes a test using a Penile Plethysmograph, which measures the extent of each offender's sexual arousal. This is followed by the Core Programme, which seeks to encourage offenders to accept active responsibility for their behaviour, to identify the particular situations, behaviours, moods and thoughts that puts each offender at risk of offending and to develop coping strategies in order to avoid re-offending. Further modules in anger management, relationships and deviancy are available as necessary and a Relapse Prevention ('booster') Programme provides an opportunity for offenders to practice the skills and behaviours required to enact their coping strategies. Overall, the Sex Offender Treatment Programme aims to reinforce the notion that offenders cannot be cured, but must constantly guard against temptation and risk.

The importance of offence related programmes for the Prison Service was highlighted recently by the setting of a Key Performance Indicator (see *Chapter 7*) for 1997-98 which sought

to ensure that there are at least 2,200 completions by prisoners of programmes accredited as being effective in reducing re-offending, of which 670 should be sex offender treatment programmes.

Release on temporary licence (ROTL)

Release on temporary licence allows certain prisoners an opportunity to re-adjust to life outside prison and to prepare for their release. As 'temporary release' and 'home leave', it was first introduced into the borstal system over 40 years ago. Prison Rule 6 states that prisoners may be released:

on compassionate grounds or for the purpose of receiving medical treatment;

to engage in employment or voluntary work;

to receive instruction or training which cannot reasonably be provided in the prison;

to enable them to participate in any proceedings before any court, tribunal or inquiry;

to enable them to consult with legal advisers in circumstances where it is not reasonably practicable for the consultation to take place in the prison;

126

to assist any police officer in any enquiries;
to facilitate the prisoner's transfer between prisons;
to assist them in maintaining family ties or in transition from prison life to
freedom;
to enable them to make a visit in the locality of the prison, as a reward for
good behaviour or performance.

Controversy over the number of prisoners abusing home
leave/temporary release—including the commission of several, very
serious crimes—was one reason why the former home secretary,
Michael Howard curtailed prisoners' access to temporary release. In
contrast, prison systems in many other countries make liberal use of
home leave as a way of preparing prisoners for their eventual release.

A Victim Helpline was introduced in 1994 to allow victims to pass
on any concerns they may have to the Prison Service about prisoners
who are granted temporary release or parole. However, to date, the
service has been used only rarely and it is unclear whether any of the
information has affected decisions to grant home leave or temporary
release.

Inmate Development Pre-release Programmes

The purpose of Inmate Development Pre-release Programmes (IDPRs)
is to help prisoners prepare for their release. Pre-release training
provides prisoners with information, advice and guidance on various
resettlement issues, including housing, work, training and benefits. The
programme may include training in job search, interviewing skills, the
completion of application forms and preparation of a curriculum vitae.
Where appropriate, use is made of outside speakers. The programme is
normally available to prisoners about six weeks before they are due to
be released.

Because the funding for IDPR courses is included within the
education budget, many courses have had to be reduced or abandoned
in recent years.

DISCHARGE GRANTS

In 1963, the Advisory Council on the Treatment of Offenders proposed
that all prisoners should be provided with a small amount of money on
release to tide them over the time it takes to apply for and receive social
security benefits. Not all prisoners are entitled to the grant and the
amount varies depending on age and whether discharged prisoners
have a home to go to. Prisoners who do not have a home to go to and
must move into a hostel or lodgings, or have tried and failed to find

accommodation, receive a higher discharge grant. Prisoners are not entitled to a discharge grant if they are under the age of 16, if they are serving less than 15 days in prison for fine default, or if they have savings of over £8,000.

Although it takes about a fortnight for discharged prisoners to receive their first payment from the DSS, the discharge grant is only equivalent to one week's benefit entitlement.

CHAPTER 7

Staffing, Management and Accountability

Prisons in England and Wales are run by HM Prison Service, an agency of the Home Office. The agency itself is run by a Prisons Board, chaired by the director general. With the exception of those employed by private prison operators, all staff are civil servants.

The Prison Act 1952 is the legislative authority governing prisons and imprisonment. It vests authority over prisons in the home secretary, who is accountable to Parliament for them. It is the primary duty of the home secretary to ensure that sufficient prisons and staff are available and that basic conditions and standards are complied with.

Policy and performance targets are set by the home secretary, with advice from the Home Office's permanent secretary and the director general. The director general is responsible for the day-to-day management of the Prison Service and is accountable to the home secretary for implementing policy and maintaining performance.

The total annual cost of the Prison Service to tax payers is around £1.8 billion. The annual cost per prisoner place is about £24,000. The cost of imprisonment varies considerably depending on the level of security required for each prisoner. For the period April 1997 to December 1997, the average cost per week for keeping a prisoner in a dispersal prison was £677; a category B, category C and local prison was £337; an open prison was £291; and a young offender institution was £346.

INTERNAL STRUCTURE

The internal structure of the prison system consists of 139 prisons supported by a headquarters responsible for determining strategy, servicing and supporting the work of individual prisons.

Within headquarters, the director general of the Prison Service is supported by the Prisons Board. The Prisons Board is comprised of eight directorates: Operations (North), Operations (South), Personnel, Finance, Health Care, Services Delivery, Dispersals and Regimes. In addition, there is a deputy director general and a number of non-executive members, of whom currently there are three.

Twelve area managers provide the link between the Prisons Board and individual prison establishments. Each area manager is responsible for managing and supporting prison governors to maintain

129

performance in up to 13 prisons. Their role is to ensure prisons are developed in line with national priorities and expectations.

THE PRISON ACT 1952

The Prison Act 1952 is a brief statute and its provisions are expressed in general terms. It places few obligations upon the prison authorities and asserts few entitlements on the part of prisoners. For instance, although the 1952 Act requires the home secretary to ensure the provision of sufficient accommodation it does not prohibit overcrowding. The Act also does not confer upon prisoners the right to sue for breach of a statutory duty.

The lack of regulations to which prisons must adhere and which are legally enforceable has raised questions about the need for more specific standards for the running of prisons. The Woolf Report recommended a national system of accredited standards with which prisons would be required to comply. There have also been calls for a new Prison Act containing statutory minimum standards, guaranteeing access to work, education etc. The Prison Service has promulgated a Code of Operating Standards, but its terms are advisory and aspirational rather than guaranteed levels of performance and service.

PRISON RULES

The Prison Rules 1964 provide the regulatory framework for the treatment of prisoners in England and Wales. Separate Young Offender Institution Rules were introduced in 1988. The Prison Rules are a statutory instrument under the Prison Act 1952, section 47(1) of which requires the home secretary to provide rules for the

> regulation and management of prisons . . . and for the classification, treatment, employment, discipline and control of persons required to be detained therein.

Like the Prison Act itself, the Prison Rules provide regulatory directions only. The wording of certain rules—'so far as reasonably practicable'; 'subject to any directions of the secretary of state'—mean that they leave a range of important matters to the discretion of the prison authorities.

European Prison Rules
Just as the United Kingdom's domestic Prison Rules rarely provide specific entitlements, the same is true of international standards for prisons. Amongst the most important of these are the European Prison

Rules. These have nothing to do with the European Union, but have been drawn up by the Strasbourg-based Council of Europe. The Council of Europe recommends that 'governments of member states [should] be guided in their internal legislation and practice by the principles set out in the text of the European Prison Rules . . . with a view to their progressive implementation'. In other words, the European Prison Rules provide guidelines for the treatment of people in prison, but they are not directly enforceable in law.

ORDERS AND INSTRUCTIONS

Owing to the general nature of the Prison Rules they must be supplemented by other administrative guidelines and documents. These are provided in the form of Prison Service Orders and Instructions (what used to be known as Standing Orders and Circular Instructions). The Prison Service Orders are management instructions. They are issued by headquarters to detail the position on various matters, such as prisoners' letters and visits, prison discipline etc. They were made public documents in 1981 and are available to prisoners in prison libraries. Prison Service Instructions amend the Prison Service Orders where necessary and provide further detail on issues of practice.

THE STATEMENT OF PURPOSE, VISION, GOALS AND VALUES

The Statement of Purpose of the Prison Service was adopted in 1988 and is displayed in the reception area of every prison. As we saw in *Chapter 2*, it reads as follows:

> Her Majesty's Prison Service serves the public by keeping in custody those committed by the courts. Our duty is to look after them with humanity and help them lead law-abiding and useful lives in custody and after release.

The Statement of Purpose requires the Prison Service to perform a number of different, but inter-related, functions within the criminal justice system. It provides services to the courts; it is responsible for holding in custody those remanded in custody or sentenced to deprivation of liberty as a punishment; and it is concerned with the treatment and training of prisoners. Overall, the Prison Service performs a dual role: prisoners must be accommodated safely and securely and at the same time enabled to lead more fulfilling and crime-free lives after release.

As discussed previously, maintaining a balance between security and rehabilitation is a complex operation. In a revealing passage, the former chief inspector of prisons, Sir Stephen Tumim, said in an inspection report of Blantyre House prison in Kent:

> Blantyre House . . . is an unusual example of the application of the training concept to the total regime of a prison. The Prison Service Statement of Purpose is actually being followed.

For HM Chief Inspector to be surprised that a prison is actually following the Prison Service Statement of Purpose is either an indictment of the wording of the statement or an implied criticism of the ability of the Prison Service to achieve its aims.

More recently, the Learmont report of 1995 argued that there was widespread confusion and tension amongst Prison Service staff over the competing objectives of 'custody' on the one hand and 'care' on the other. Learmont suggested that, because the wording of the Statement of Purpose does not confer more importance on one aim than the other, it should be re-written to make custody the primary purpose. In response, the Home Office argued that the 'current statement of purpose already makes clear the primacy of custody'.

Such arguments are characteristic of the uncertainty which surrounds the overall purpose of prisons. Is it feasible to expect the Prison Service to contain prisoners securely and at the same time bring about their reformation as law abiding citizens? Confidence in the ability of prisons to change the behaviour of offenders for the better has ebbed and flowed over the years.

Vision and values

The Prison Service in England and Wales functions as an integral part of the criminal justice system; and other parts of the system have a direct impact on its operations. For instance, the Prison Service has no control over the number of people sent to it by the courts. Even when the prison population exceeds the capacity to provide reasonable standards of accommodation, and prisons are beset with crises of security and control, the Prison Service must continue to provide a wide range of services all year round to prisoners who are held against their will. But despite a general recognition that the Prison Service performs a complex and difficult task, any failure on its part to maintain standards, provokes public alarm and intense media criticism about its work.

It was for these and other reasons that Admiral Sir Raymond Lygo, the author of a review of Prison Service management, commented in 1991 that 'the Prison Service is the most complex organization I have encountered and its problems some of the most intractable'.

In keeping with the finding of the Woolf Report that prison staff 'lack confidence in the value of what they do', the Lygo Report endorsed the need for more visible leadership, clearer priorities, the modernisation of management information systems and more autonomy for individual prison governors.

Of crucial importance to the new arrangements was the relationship between the Prison Service and Home Office ministers. Lygo insisted that, once the policies and priorities had been set, it was essential for the Prison Service to get on with the job of running prisons free from ministerial interference. To achieve an appropriate degree of independence, Lygo recommended that the Prison Service should become a 'Next Steps' executive agency of government, with a director general appointed to run operations and assume responsibility for overall performance. The effect of this would be to diminish the involvement of ministers in day-to-day operations and confer upon the Prison Service far greater control over its affairs. Although the Prison Service would be subject to the strategy developed by the home secretary, in future it would be for the Prison Service agency to decide how to meet these strategic objectives.

As was noted earlier, the Prison Service became a 'Next Steps' agency on 1 April 1993. Derek Lewis, the first director general of the new agency, was appointed from a background in finance (his main jobs had been with Ford, Granada, the television and hotels group, and UK Gold, the cable television company of which he remained chairman). His private sector experience was meant to provide new ways of working, a break from the traditional approach of the Whitehall mandarin.

The Prison Service agency now operates within terms set out in a specially prepared framework document. The framework includes the Statement of Purpose, which is supplemented by a vision, six goals and five core values. It also includes planning, financial and personnel arrangements, descriptions of the responsibilities of the home secretary, the permanent secretary of state for the Home Office and the director general of the Prison Service, and details of the various mechanisms by which the Prison Service is held accountable to Parliament and to the general public.

The vision of the Prison Service agency is as follows:

Our vision is to provide a service, through both directly managed and contracted prisons, of which the public can be proud and which will be regarded as a standard of excellence around the world.

Its principal goals are to:

keep prisoners in custody;

maintain order, control, discipline and a safe environment;

provide decent conditions for prisoners and meet their needs, including health care;

provide positive regimes which help prisoners address their offending behaviour and allow them as full and responsible a life as possible;

help prisoners prepare for their return to the community;

deliver prison services using the resources provided by Parliament with maximum efficiency.

The Prison Service is enjoined to adhere to the following values:

Integrity is fundamental to everything we do. We will meet our legal obligations, act with honesty and openness, and exercise effective stewardship of public money and assets.

Commitment by our staff and to our staff are the most important assets of the Prison Service. They will be empowered to develop and use their skills and abilities to the full, while being held accountable for their performance. Teamwork will be encouraged. They will be treated with fairness, respect and openness. Their safety and well-being will be a prime concern.

Care for prisoners. Prisoners will be treated with fairness, justice and respect as individuals. Their punishment is deprivation of liberty and they are entitled to certain recognised standards while in prison. They will be given reasons for decisions and, where possible, involved in discussions about matters affecting them. In working with prisoners, we will involve their families and others in the community as fully as possible.

Equality of opportunity. We are committed to equality of opportunity and the elimination of discrimination on improper grounds.

Innovation and improvement are essential to the success of the service, requiring the acceptance of change and the delivery of continuing improvements in quality and efficiency.

Key Performance Indicators (KPIs)

Agency status has also required the Prison Service to publish separate corporate and business plans which identify clear targets and establish key performance indicators (KPIs) against which the performance of the agency can be measured. Such techniques have been part of management practice within the private sector for some time, but it was only with the advent of agency status that they have been employed comprehensively within the Prison Service.

The Prison Service performance targets for 1997-1998 covered the following areas:

134

- the number of escapes from prison establishments and from escorts;
- the number of assaults on staff, prisoners and others which result in a disciplinary adjudication;
- the number of drug tests that prove positive;
- the proportion of prisoners held in units of accommodation intended for fewer numbers;
- the number of hours a week which, on average, prisoners spend in purposeful activity;
- the proportion of prisoners held in establishments where prisoners not on the basic regime are unlocked on weekdays for a total of at least 10 hours;
- the number of completions by prisoners of programmes accredited as being effective in reducing re-offending;
- the average cost per prisoner place;
- the amount of time staff spend in training.

In 1994-1995, the Prison Service met all of its performance targets. Escapes fell by 18 per cent, assaults fell by six per cent, no prisoners were held three to a cell and targets for access to sanitation, hours out-of-cell and in 'purposeful' activity, visiting entitlements and costs were all achieved. During the year 1996-97, as a consequence of increasing pressures on the prison system, only eight of the 11 performance targets were achieved. In 1997-1998, all targets were achieved with the exception of a reduction in the number of assaults.

Commenting on the publication of the performance results for 1997-98, Joyce Quin, the then prisons and probation minister, said:

> The Prison Service has produced an outstanding performance in what has been a challenging year. The government has supported the service by providing additional resources to cope with the continuing increase in prisoner numbers, but the way staff have met the increased demands made of them has been magnificent.

However, opinion has been divided over the effectiveness of KPIs to measure performance accurately. There are obvious difficulties in identifying the most appropriate KPIs for an organization as complex as the Prison Service. Staff may not agree about what are the most important goals. Measuring performance in a quantitative way does not necessarily give an indication of quality. Targets which cover general areas of work can be measured using different KPIs—for example, helping prisoners return to the community is not achieved solely by providing more than the minimum visiting entitlements—it is also achieved by enabling prisoners to gain education qualifications, or by helping them find accommodation after release. The data provided is not always accurate. Performance targets may be set too high or too low.

Although the general view of the new Prison Service agency has been favourable, there have been some criticisms expressed. The escape of high security prisoners from Parkhurst and Whitemoor, strong criticisms of management contained within the Learmont report and the subsequent sacking of Derek Lewis as director general, have all raised questions about the effectiveness of the agency.

In particular, criticisms made by Derek Lewis about the way the former home secretary, Michael Howard, interfered with day-to-day operational matters within the Prison Service have focused attention on the relationship between the Prison Service agency and the Home Office and the degree to which real autonomy for the Prison Service has been achieved. However, in March 1997, the House of Commons Home Affairs Committee published a report into the management of the service in which they concluded that agency status has 'undoubtedly introduced a dynamism into what some of us remember to have been a uniformly old-fashioned, cumbersome and inefficient structure'.

Relations between ministers and officials have improved somewhat since the new home secretary, Jack Straw, announced measures to assert and reinforce proper ministerial responsibility for the Prison Service. These include a renewal of ministerial responsibility for the answering of Parliamentary Questions (under the previous administration these had been answered by the head of the Prison Service) and quarterly meetings chaired by ministers to review performance and plans.

STAFFING

The Prison Act 1952 requires that 'every prison shall have a governor, a chaplain and a medical officer and such other officers as may be necessary'. There are up to eight grades between the basic grade officer and the 'number one' governor.

Staffing levels are high compared to American prisons, but low compared to some in Europe. On 31 March 1998, 41,054 staff were employed by the Prison Service, of whom 23,444 were prison officers and 17,610 were other staff, including governors, specialist grades like psychologists and staff at headquarters. The ratio between all staff and prisoners at this time was 1 to 1.33.

Nearly 7,000 staff (18 per cent) are women and just over 1,000 (2.5 per cent) are from ethnic minorities. Despite the disproportionate number of black prisoners—as we have seen, about one fifth of the prison population are from ethnic minorities—black prison officers and governors are badly under-represented amongst prison staff. Presently, there are only nine black officers who have attained the grade of principal officer and only six junior governors have been appointed. The London prisons have been more successful in recruiting black staff. But some prisons, including—surprisingly—Liverpool and Cardiff, have no black or Asian officers at all.

Depending on whether they are employed in an operational or administrative capacity, Prison Service staff are represented by a number of different trades unions. As we have seen in *Chapter 1*, the two most important are the Prison Governors Association (PGA) which represents prison governors and the Prison Officers Association (POA) which represents the vast majority of the uniformed officer grades.

As small self-contained communities, charged with helping prisoners 'to lead law-abiding and useful lives in custody and after release', prison staff are required to provide a wide range of services and to perform a wide variety of tasks. All prison staff, in one way or another, must deal with the day-to-day domestic needs of prisoners and provide them with a range of training and treatment programmes. For this reason, the Prison Service employs staff who have been trained in a large number of different disciplines.

Each prison is like a small town. As well as the core prison staff, which is made up of administrators, governors and prison officers, the Prison Service employs non-uniformed specialist staff, including teachers, physical education instructors, doctors, nurses, psychologists, chaplains, industrial managers, catering and maintenance staff. In addition, as was discussed in more detail in *Chapter 6*, probation officers are seconded from local probation services to help prepare prisoners for release and staff from voluntary organizations provide a variety of counselling and advice services.

PRISON GOVERNORS

There are up to five governor grades responsible for all aspects of prison management. The 'governing governor', or 'number one governor', has overall responsibility for operational management and is accountable to headquarters for performance. The governing governor must provide strong leadership, be able to respond effectively in times of crisis and achieve results in line with the overall goals of the Prison Service. Since 1993, governors have also been responsible for directly managing more and more of their budgets. Governor grades below the number one governor are responsible for the management of parts of the prison or for aspects of the regime.

Although a series of management reviews have changed the role and responsibilities of prison governors in recent years, it remains an essential part of the governor's job to walk the landings and to develop good working relationships with both staff and prisoners. Similar to the captain of a ship, prison governors can strongly influence the atmosphere in prisons by the way they conduct themselves and relate to prisoners and staff.

PRISON OFFICERS

The need for prison staff to perform a wide variety of tasks is most apparent in the work of prison officers. They must ensure prisons are kept secure and well controlled. They must also develop good quality relationships with prisoners—a concept sometimes referred to as 'dynamic security'. The everyday tasks that prison officers perform depend to a large extent on the type and category of prison in which they work. For instance, the primary responsibility of prison officers in high security prisons is to carry out strict security procedures and routines to prevent offenders escaping or causing disturbances. At the other extreme, prison officers in open prisons, where the need for tight security is less relevant, are more concerned with preparing prisoners for release. In addition, prison officers who work in womens' prisons, young offender institutions, or prisons which contain a high proportion of sex offenders, must be able to respond to their particular needs.

Notwithstanding such differences, many of the basic tasks performed by prison officers are common to all prisons. Prison officers must:

- enforce discipline, but also provide support to prisoners;
- ensure that prisons are secure and that prisoners who transgress prison rules are dealt with firmly and professionally. They have the power, if necessary, to restrain prisoners; and yet, at the same time must also
- help prepare prisoners for their freedom.

Traditionally, work in prisons has been performed by men, many of whom had come from a military background. In recent years efforts have been made to change the profile of prison officers by employing an increasing number of women and by recruiting from a wider range of previous occupations.

All prison officers must be over 19 and a half years of age, but many officers join the Prison Service in their 30s as a second career. Prison officers can earn up to £20,499 per annum, which can rise to £24,643 per annum on becoming a principal officer.

Custody duties

First and foremost, prison officers must ensure that prisoners are kept safely and securely. Every day, prison officers have to carry out routine security duties such as locking and unlocking doors, counting prisoners, walking the landings, searching cells, prisoners and visitors and escorting prisoners from one part of the prison to another.

In order to ensure that prisons are staffed 24 hours a day, prison officers work a shift system which is usually divided into an early, main and late shift. Prison officers working the main shift usually arrive for work at about 7.30 a.m. After collecting their keys, they pass through the main security gate to the locker rooms where they change from civilian clothes into standard prison uniforms. From there they walk to the wings or landings where they receive information from officers on the early shift about any incidents which may have occurred during the night. They are also told about any prisoners who need to be unlocked at specific times of the day so that they can attend court hearings, or visit the health care centre.

Throughout the day prison officers carry out roll checks to ensure all prisoners are present and accounted for. Usually, these take place before and after meal times and after prisoners have returned to their cells from working or attending education in other parts of the prison. After tea, at about 4.30 p.m., the main shift hands over to the late shift.

Staff/prisoner relationships

Routine is essential to the safe running of prisons. However, safety in prison does not rely solely on prison officers carrying out standard security procedures. It also relies on prison officers establishing good working relationships with prisoners and getting to know them as individuals. Staff and prisoners live cheek by jowl with one another. Security and control may be jeopardised if relationships become strained. Good staff/prisoner relations underpin 'dynamic security' and are crucial to the maintenance of good order and the development of constructive prison regimes.

It is frequently said of prison officers that they need to be firm but fair. But they also need to be sensitive to the needs of vulnerable prisoners, to support those who are unable to cope with prison life and who may be suicidal. They need to be able to empathise with prisoners, to resolve their problems, to respond to their requests for help and to involve outside agencies as appropriate.

Although prison officers are primarily concerned with security and control, many of them want to shake off their image as warders or 'turnkeys' and to take on a much wider range of responsibilities. For example, prison officers now contribute to treatment programmes and the aftercare of prisoners. They are responsible for Inmate Development and Pre-release Training, anti-bullying, anger management and drugs awareness programmes; and they are closely involved in sentence planning, assessing the needs of prisoners and monitoring their progress. Prison officers also write reports on prisoners which are used to assess their eligibility for release on temporary licence and parole.

Training

The need for prison officers to be trained in a wide variety of disciplines was acknowledged formally for the first time in 1984, when a review of prison officer training was set up to analyse the prison officer's job and to identify the various skills and aptitudes required. The review found that the way prison officers conduct themselves determines the atmosphere in prisons and that insensitive officers could easily provoke prisoner hostility. The review concluded that prison officers should be assertive without being hostile, and helpful and understanding without becoming over involved emotionally.

Since 1984, interactive skills training has been provided for all new entrant prison officers. Previous to this, prison officer training consisted mostly of technical information, with a few add-on sessions exploring the causes of crime and the purposes of punishment.

Today, the minimum educational requirement for new prison officers is five GCSEs, although this does not necessarily apply to all the privately managed prisons, some of which require no formal educational qualifications. In addition, people who apply to become prison officers must first undergo a rigorous assessment process to gauge whether they are suitable for the job. This is done through continuous monitoring, testing, practical exercises and assessments carried out during interviews. Suitable candidates then progress to the training stage.

Initial training consists of nine weeks at the Prison Service Training College, followed by two weeks in-service training at a prison. The training covers a broad spectrum of areas including reception duties, search, control and restraint techniques and racism awareness training. Once prison officers begin work proper, training in specialised areas continues.

The Prison Service has committed itself to providing all prison officers with at least six in-service training days per year and to helping them gain national vocational qualifications in transferable skills. In addition, some prison officers receive continuation training centrally at the Prison Service Training College in order to equip them to take on certain specialist roles.

Personal officers
Personal officers are trained to work closely with a small group of prisoners, to help them adjust to prison life and to address any concerns they may have. On a more formal basis, they assist prisoners with sentence planning, identify work and educational activities most suited to their needs and prepare progress reports for the probation service.

PROBATION OFFICERS

As set out in the *National Standards for the Supervision of Offenders in the Community* (1995), the overall aims of probation work with offenders in custody and after release are:

the rehabilitation of the offender;
the protection of the public from harm from the offender;
the prevention of further offending.

Although probation officers have worked in prisons ever since the Probation Service was established in 1907, it was not until 1966 that they were seconded on a formal basis to all prisons. Today, each prison has a small team of probation officers who help prisoners prepare for their release. On 31 December 1996 there were 543 probation officers working in prisons.

Traditionally charged with providing a welfare function to prisoners, in recent years the Probation Service has been expected to perform a more explicit throughcare role. The purpose of this is to ensure continuity for prisoners between custody and their release on licence.

ACCOUNTABILITY

In all areas of public life, systems of accountability are meant to ensure that institutions and organizations conduct themselves in a manner which accords with basic principles of justice and reasonableness. Mechanisms have been introduced which empower citizens to seek redress for any grievances they may have. Most recently, the *Citizen's Charter* initiative has made more information available about what can be expected from public services and has enabled individuals to complain or demand compensation when they are not treated properly.

By their very nature prisons are closed worlds. In order to function securely, prisoners are required to adhere to a rigid set of rules which govern their rights and activities. All aspects of their daily lives are watched over and regulated by prison staff. The manner in which they are treated—what time they get up in the morning, what they eat, who they can talk to—is strictly regulated and controlled. Because a precondition of effective security and control is a degree of secrecy, traditionally prisoners have been denied the most basic information relating to their imprisonment and the work of the Prison Service has remained impervious to close public scrutiny.

The lack of information concerning what goes on behind prison walls has provoked frequent criticism of the Prison Service for being inflexible and overly protective regarding its activities. It has also been suggested that openness is a precursor of good prison management. Lord Woolf cited a lack of accountability in prisons as a major factor in provoking feelings of injustice amongst prisoners, which in turn contribute to the threat of disorder and rioting. Indeed, it has been argued that prisons cannot function without the prior consent and co-operation of prisoners. Prisoners may be frustrated by the general conditions in which they are kept—the quality of prison food or the state of prison buildings are frequent sources of complaint—or by decisions which affect them personally, for example, those regarding the segregation or transfer of disruptive prisoners, parole, or punishments such as loss of privileges or the imposition of 'added days' resulting from disciplinary hearings. This feeling of frustration may be exacerbated if prisoners are 'kept in the dark' and denied information or explanation regarding decisions which affect them personally.

It was for this reason that the Woolf Report called for prisons to be made more 'permeable' to outside scrutiny. The report also sought a system of greater internal accountability; in particular, Woolf said prisoners had a right to be told the reasons for decisions, especially those decisions which affected them adversely.

The public receives information about the prison system from various sources. The Prison Service publishes an *Annual Report* and a wide variety of statistical information is also available. Research is commissioned both internally and from the Universities. The Home Affairs Select Committee reports regularly to Parliament on various aspects of the prison system. Parliamentary Questions are regularly posed and answered. In addition, reports are sent to the home secretary by Her Majesty's Chief Inspector of Prisons and by prison Boards of Visitors.

142

However, such reports on their own do not always provide information in a way which is easily understandable to either prisoners or the general public.

As a means of making the prison system more 'permeable' to a greater degree of public understanding, the Woolf Report recommended that prisons should play a greater role in the communities in which they are situated. In particular, the development of a 'community prison' system, as Woolf termed it, would enable prisoners to be kept in prisons as close to their homes as possible and give them the opportunity to work for charitable causes and to participate in local sporting activities etc. In turn, local community organizations would become more involved in the day-to-day operations of prisons. As a means of establishing a coherent system of prisoners' rights, the Woolf Report called for the introduction of new grievance procedures, the establishment of a complaints adjudicator (later known as a Prisons Ombudsman) and the development of prisoner contracts.

Grievance procedures

Prisoners can use a variety of procedures to seek redress for any grievances they may have.

Internal prison procedures require prisoners to discuss grievances with wing or landing officers or, if appropriate, with prison governors. Those prisoners not satisfied with the outcome may then submit a written request or complaint to the prison governor or a senior member of staff to which they are entitled to a written reply. The reply should provide details of the action taken, or explain why the request or complaint has been refused. Prisoners who remain dissatisfied may then appeal directly to an area manager, or they may write to their MPs, to outside organizations like the Prison Reform Trust, to the Commission for Racial Equality, or to their lawyers. Finally, they may ask for their case to be reviewed by the Prisons Ombudsman.

Prisons Ombudsman

The establishment of a Prisons Ombudsman is a relatively recent development. The post (then known as complaints adjudicator) was recommended by Lord Woolf in response to the lack of confidence in which the internal complaints procedure was held by a majority of prisoners. Woolf noted that

Within a prison in particular, it is an important requirement of justice that justice should not only actually be done but should be seen to be done. It will not be seen to be done if there is no proper procedure, if there are no established rules, if the prisoner is not made aware of those rules, and if there is not, at least at the final stage of the process, recourse to an independent element.

In 1994 the first Prisons Ombudsman, Sir Peter Woodhead, formerly the deputy supreme allied commander in the Atlantic, was appointed. His remit is to investigate individual grievances and act as the final avenue of appeal against findings at disciplinary hearings.

Before the Ombudsman can proceed with an investigation, prisoners must have pursued their complaint through the internal request and complaint procedures. If it is considered there is a case to answer, the Ombudsman can investigate all matters affecting prisoners, excluding those which are the subject of litigation or criminal proceedings, or involve the actions of bodies outside the Prison Service (e.g. the courts, police, Immigration Service, DSS, and the Parole Board). The Ombudsman also has no authority over ministerial decisions affecting the release of mandatory life sentenced prisoners.

The Ombudsman has the power to make recommendations only. He cannot make executive decisions and he cannot award compensation—although in some cases he may recommend *ex gratia* payments.

During the first year of operation the Ombudsman received 2,050 complaints, 424 of which were investigated and 44 per cent upheld.

Boards of Visitors (BoVs)
Since the interests of security dictate that prisons cannot be freely accessible to the public, it falls on BoVs to take on a watchdog role and report on the condition of prisons and the treatment of prisoners.

Boards of Visitors are made up of ordinary members of the public, at least two of whom must be magistrates. The average board membership is 13. A National Advisory Council represents BoVs on a national basis and organizes training for members.

Formally, BoVs have very extensive powers. The Prison Act 1952 empowers Board members 'at any time [to] enter the prison and . . . have free access to every part of it and to every prisoner' and 'to pay frequent visits to the prison and hear any complaints which may be made by the prisoners'. Prison Rule 94(1) states that the principal duty of boards is to satisfy themselves 'as to the state of the prison premises, the administration of the prison and the treatment of prisoners'. Each board produces an annual report which it submits to the secretary of state, and which it may publish. Sadly, despite encouragement from the Home Office, only a minority of boards currently publish their reports.

For most of their history, BoVs also carried out adjudications on prisoners charged with serious breaches of prison discipline. From 1 April 1992, BoVs ceased to have any disciplinary role because it was considered inconsistent with their 'watchdog' responsibilities. In his report, Lord Woolf recommended that the watchdog role of BoVs should be enhanced.

However, the question remains whether a body of lay people can, in their spare time, carry out a satisfactory watchdog role in prisons. Research published in the *British Journal of Criminology* in 1994 showed that BoVs were

> still regarded by most inmates as largely invisible, irrelevant, aligned with the prison management, and ineffective. Inmates had little confidence in Boards of Visitors.

Whether this is a fair characterisation or not—each year, between them, BoV members make hundreds of visits to each prison—it is doubtful if prisoners today would reach a different conclusion.

Prisoners' contracts

The Woolf Report recommended that a contract or compact should be drawn up by the Prison Service setting out what prisoners could legitimately expect prisons to provide for them during their sentence. In return, the prisoner would comply with the expectations and responsibilities the contract placed upon him or her. Although such contracts would have no special legal status, Woolf thought they might prove useful and influential. Many prisons now offer such contracts which include minimum standards of accommodation and regime activities and may be reviewed yearly to take account of any progress made by the prisoner.

Although contracts provide a structure for deciding on the programmes and activities most suitable to individual prisoners—akin to sentence planning—and certainly improve the flow and quality of information to prisoners, they may represent a commitment on paper only. Prisoners have no right of redress if the terms of the contract are not met. Indeed, some prisoners have been punished for refusing to sign contracts they know they cannot enforce.

Her Majesty's Inspectorate of Prisons

The Prison Act 1952 provides for the appointment of inspectors of prisons whose duty it is to inspect, or to arrange for the inspection of, prisons in England and Wales and to report on them to the secretary of state, in particular on the treatment of prisoners and on conditions within prisons. It is also the duty of HM Chief Inspector of Prisons to report to the secretary of state on specific matters as required, and to submit an annual report to be laid before Parliament.

An independent inspector of prisons was first established on 1 January 1981, following a recommendation by the May Committee. Previously, the Prison Service carried out its own internal inspections and produced reports which were confidential to the Prisons Board. Since 1981, HM Chief Inspector of Prisons has opened up the prison system to unprecedented public scrutiny and a series of influential and highly critical reports have been issued.

Although part of the Home Office and answerable to the home secretary, HM Chief Inspector of Prisons, as a statutory Crown officer, maintains independence from government by making unannounced visits to prisons and publishing all reports in full (with the exception of security findings and recommendations). In addition, although inspection teams are comprised for the most part of staff seconded from within the Prison Service, they also include a number of outside guest inspectors.

All prisons should be subject to a full inspection every five years, which on average takes one week to complete. In order to meet the statutory requirement of covering all 139 prisons, 27 inspections must be carried out every year. Complementing longer inspections are short unannounced inspections, which assess progress and follow up recommendations made in previous visits.

The chief inspector also produces reports which comment on wider issues facing the Prison Service. An example is the report by Sir James Hennessy into the series of prison riots in 1986. Similarly, following a rise in the number of suicides particularly of young prisoners, Sir Stephen Tumim produced an authoritative report on suicide prevention. The current chief inspector, Sir David Ramsbotham has continued to highlight issues of concern by publishing thematic reports on healthcare, women prisoners and young offenders. Reviews of the lifer system and suicide prevention have also been started and one on the work of local prisons is planned.

Pressure groups

One other form of accountability in prisons results from the unofficial activities of the penal pressure groups. The United Kingdom is perhaps unique in the strength and vigour of its penal reform lobby. Three main organizations campaign for change in prison policy and aim to increase public understanding of how the prison system operates. The three—the Prison Reform Trust, NACRO and the Howard League for Penal Reform—also carry out research and offer information.

The Prison Reform Trust (PRT) was established in 1981 and is the youngest of the penal reform groups. PRT produces a quarterly magazine, *Prison Report*, which is free to prisoners, runs a writing

146

competition for prisoners and, since 1990, has published, jointly with the Prison Service, the *Prisoners' Information Book* which gives prisoners advice and guidance about the terms of their imprisonment.

The National Association for the Care and Resettlement of Offenders (NACRO) grew out of the National Association of Discharged Prisoners' Aid Societies and was established formally in 1966. Today, it is the largest of the voluntary organizations working in the penal sphere, employing just under 1,000 staff on various employment training, crime prevention and prisoner resettlement programmes. NACRO's Prison Link Unit trains prison officers to give advice on housing and employment issues to prisoners approaching release.

The Howard League for Penal Reform was founded in 1921 and is the oldest of the three organizations. Named after John Howard, the influential penal reformer who brought the appalling state of prisons to the attention of the government throughout the later part of the eighteenth century (see *Chapter 2*), the Howard League for Penal Reform produces a quarterly magazine, *Criminal Justice,* which is free to prisoners and the more academic *Howard Journal* which analyses aspects of the criminal justice system in detail.

Perhaps ironically, an increasingly important function of the penal reform lobby in recent years has been to act as a sort of unofficial Public Relations Department for the Prison Service. Improvements in openness stemming from the Woolf Report have not always eased the defensive attitude the Prison Service presents to the media. Jon Silverman, Home Affairs Correspondent for the BBC, has commented:

> There is little sense of any grand strategy for peeling back some of the layers of secrecy which keep our gaols from public scrutiny. It's small wonder that many journalists turn to the Prison Reform Trust or the Howard League for insights into the prison system rather than the service itself.

Suggestions for Further Reading

General

Cavadino, M and Dignan, J (1997), *The Penal System: An Introduction*, Sage

Leech M, *The Prisons Handbook*, Waterside Press, 1998 (Third edition)

Liebling, A (1998), *Deaths of Offenders: The Hidden Side of Justice*, Waterside Press

Maguire, M, Morgan, R and Reiner, R (Eds.) (1996), *The Oxford Handbook of Criminology*, Oxford University Press

Morris, N and Rothman, D (Eds.) (1995), *The Oxford History of the Prison: The Practice of Punishment in Western Society*, Oxford University Press

Pettifer E (1939), *Punishments of Former Days*, Waterside Press (reprinted 1992)

Ruggerio, V, Ryan, M and Sim, J (Eds) (1995), *Western European Prison Systems: A Critical Anatomy*, Sage

Stern, V (1998), *A Sin Against The Future: Imprisonment in the World*, Penguin

Stern, V (1987), *Bricks of Shame: Britain's Prisons*, Penguin

Woolf, H and Tumim, S (1991), *Prison Disturbances April 1990*, Cm 1456, HMSO

Personal Accounts

Behan, B (1958), *Borstal Boy*, Hutchinson

Boyle, J (1977), *A Sense of Freedom*, Pan Books

Leech, M (1992), *A Product Of The System*, Victor Gollancz

Turney, B (1997), *I'm Still Standing*, Waterside Press

Wilde, O (1898), *The Ballad of Reading Gaol*

On Prison Privatisation

Harding, R (1997), *Private Prisons and Public Accountability*, Open University Press

James, A, Bottomley, A, Leibling, A and Clare, E (1997), *Privatising Prisons: Rhetoric And Reality*, Sage

Ryan, M and Ward, T (1989), *Privatisation and the Penal System*, Open University Press

Shichor, D (1995), *Punishment for Profit: Private Prisons/Public Concerns*, Sage

On Women in Prison

Carlen, P (1990), *Alternatives to Women's Imprisonment*, Open University Press

Carlen, P (1998), *Sledgehammer: Women's Imprisonment at the Millennium*, Macmillan

Devlin A (1998), *Invisible Women: What's Wrong With Women's Prisons*, Waterside Press

HM Chief Inspector Of Prisons (1997), *Women In Prison: A Thematic Review*, Home Office

Morris, A, Wilkinson, C, Tisi, A, *et al* (1995), *Managing the Needs of Female Prisoners*, Home Office

On Young Offenders

HM Chief Inspector of Prisons (1997), *Young Prisoners: A Thematic Review*, Home Office

Some Useful Publications from the Prison Reform Trust

General

The Woolf Report: A Summary of the Main Findings and Recommendations of the Inquiry into Prison Disturbances

Restoring Relationships: The Purpose of Prisons by Dr George Carey, Archbishop of Canterbury.

Gladstone at 100: Essays on the Past and Future of the Prison System

Education in Prisons: A National Survey

Report of the Committee on Local Monitoring of Prison Establishments

150

A Good and Useful Life: Constructive Prison Regimes

Report of the Committee on the Penalty for Homicide

Prison Rules: A Working Guide

Prison Bill 1996: A Draft Bill to Amend the Law Relating to Prisons and the Rights of Prisoners

Comments on the White Paper "Protecting The Public": The Government's Strategy on Crime in England and Wales, March 1996

House of Commons Home Affairs Committee: Inquiry into the Management of the Prison Service (Private and Public). Submission by the Prison Reform Trust

Women in Prison: Recent Trends and Developments

Fair Votes for Prisoners

Boot Camps: Return of the Short, Sharp, Shock

Fear In Prisons: A Discussion Paper

Does Prison Work?

The Prison Population in Britain and Europe

Prisoners on Remand

Sentencing: A Geographical Lottery

Electronic Tagging: Viable Option or Expensive Diversion?

Justice for The Young: The Prison Reform Trust Annual Lecture 1997, Lord Bingham of Cornhill, Lord Chief Justice Of England

A Case for a Royal Commission on Crime and Punishment

Chain Reactions: The Shackling of Prisoners

"An Expensive Way Of Making Bad People Worse": Custody v. Community Sentencing

Facts and Figures. Three leaflets on *Men, Women* and *Young Offenders*

Race Equality in Prisons: The Role of the Race Relations Liaison Officer

Alternatives to Prison

151

Drug Use in Prison

On Achieving Prisons

Resettlement Prisons: Fulfilling the Prison Service National Statement of Purpose

Lancaster Farms: Preventing The Next Victim

Woodhill: Innovation Under Pressure

Grendon and Future Therapeutic Communities in Prison

On Private Prisons

HM Prison Buckley Hall: The First Eighteen Months

HM Prison Doncaster: The "Doncatraz" File

Blakenhurst Briefing

Wolds Remand Prison – Contracting Out: A First Year Report

Private Prison Services In Australia: Cause For Concern

Privately Managed Prisons: At What Cost?

On American Sentencing Policy

Mandatory Minimum Sentences: The American Experience

Truth in Sentencing

Automatic Life Sentences: The Californian Experience

Balancing Sentencing Policy with Resources: Structured Sentencing in North Carolina

Delaware: A Small Wonder

Washington: The State that Invented Three Strikes

The Florida Sentencing System: A Double Edged Sword

Texas: Testing the Case for Incarceration

The Federal System: Sentencing by Numbers

Sentencing Policy in California: A Visceral Thing

Further details about all the above, along with PRT's quarterly magazine, *Prison Report*, its bulletin *Prison Privatisation Report International* and its annual essay and short story competition from:

PRT, 15 Northburgh Street, London EC1V 0JR. Tel. 0171-251 5070. Fax. 0171-251 5076. E-mail. prt@prisonreform.demon.co.uk.

Index

155

Principled Policing: Protecting the Public With Integrity John Alderson

As John Alderson demonstrates, it is all too easy for quite 'ordinary' police officers to descend into behaviour which is difficult to comprehend—as a result of working cultures, state manoeuvring and the lack of fundamental values for police work. Through his description of what he calls 'high police' and by way of worldwide examples—from Northern Ireland to Tiananmen Square, Nazi Germany to J. Edgar Hoover's days at the FBI and the British miners strike of 1984/5—the author calls for decency, fairness and morality to act as touchstones for police officers everywhere.

A central appeal of *Principiled Policing* lies with its straightforward message that "good policing" flows from sound principles. The principles that John Alderson recommends to us are bound to notions of justice, fairness, tolerance and a deep sense of community. He has been preaching these principles for many years. We have not always had the sense to listen. As we enter an era in which criminal justice policy is re-built around a concern for 'social exclusion' and a heavy commitment to social crime prevention and 'partnership', we should go back to the writings of John Alderson. He was right all along. From the *Foreword* by **Professor Stephen Savage**, University of Portsmouth

John Alderson CBE, QPM, barrister-at-law is a police writer and scholar whose work is of international repute. His books and papers have been translated into many languages (from Icelandic to Chinese) and are in use in police institutions worldwide. He was formerly Chief Constable of Devon and Cornwall.

(1998) ISBN 1 872 870 71 6. £18 plus £1.50 p&p

Drugs, Trafficking and Criminal Policy: The Scapegoat Strategy Penny Green

A survey of drugs policy which explores the actual nature of events by focusing on drug trafficking and drug traffickers. Penny Green demonstrates that the vast majority of people arrested, convicted and imprisoned for drug trafficking offences are low-level players—causing her to argue that scapegoating has played a central role in shaping the criminal justice drugs war. It is those people at the bottom end of the drugs trade who give substance to its ideology and reality. The author argues that unless drug control moves beyond its present emphasis—and beyond criminal policy and law enforcement into the arena of geo-political analysis, international poverty, Third World debt and domestic welfare—there can be no resolution to the human tragedy which the war on drugs has come to embody.

Penny Green is Director of the Institute of Criminal Justice at the University of Southampton and a Senior Lecturer in Law.

(1998) ISBN 1 872 870 33 3. £18 plus £1.50 p&p

The Waterside Press Introductory Series

📖 **Introduction to the Criminal Justice Process** Bryan Gibson and Paul Cavadino. A complete overview of criminal justice. *Rarely, if ever, has this complex process been described with such comprehensiveness and clarity Justice of the Peace* (Reprinted 1997) ISBN 1 872 870 09 0. £12

📖 **Introduction to the Magistrates' Court** Bryan Gibson With a *Glossary of Words, Phrases and Abbreviations. An ideal introduction Law Society Gazette.* (1995) ISBN 1 872 870 15 5. £12. **A new enhanced third edition including** *Basic Procedures and Evidence* **is scheduled for early 1999.**

📖 **Introduction to the Youth Court** Winston Gordon, Michael Watkins and Philip Cuddy. **Foreword: Lord Woolf, Master of the Rolls** A must for those interested in the work of the youth courts *The Magistrate.* Extremely useful and practical *The Law.* (1996) ISBN 1 872 870 36 8. £12. **A new enhanced second edition is scheduled for early 1999.**

📖 **Introduction to the Probation Service** Dick Whitfield. A fully updated second edition of Anthony Osler's original work, including the Prisons/Probation Review and the effects of the Crime and Disorder Act 1998. (1998) ISBN 1 872 870 73 2 £12

📖 **Introduction to Prisons and Imprisonment** Nick Flynn **Foreword: Lord Hurd.** Under the auspices of the Prison Reform Trust. ISBN 1 872 870 37 6. £12

📖 **Introduction to Criminology** Russell Pond A basic guide for lay people written with those working in the criminal justice arena in mind. The main strands of criminology and their sources. ISBN 1 872 870 42 2. £12

📖 **Introduction to the Scottish Childrens Panel** Alistair Kelly Very interesting reading *The Law.* ISBN 1 872 870 38 4. £12.

📖 **Introduction to Road Traffic Offences** Winston Gordon, Philip Cuddy (1998) ISBN 1 872 870 51 1. £12

📖 **Introduction to the Family Proceedings Court** Elaine Laken, Chris Bazell and Winston Gordon. **Foreword: Sir Stephen Brown.** Because of its clarity of information and its lucidity of language and explanation *Introduction to the Family Proceedings Court* is a very accessible handbook *The Magistrate.* (1997) ISBN 1 872 870 46 5. £12

📖 **Conflict Resolution: A Basic Guide** Susan Stewart A wide ranging look at constructive ways of resolving disputes. ISBN 1 872 870 65 1 £12

An invaluable resource